SIX MINIATURES

SIX MINIATURES

EACH FOR
FIVE LADIES

BY

Dan Sutherland

ISIS
LARGE PRINT
MAINSTREAM SERIES
Oxford, England
Santa Barbara, California

Published in Large Print 1987 by Clio Press Ltd.,
55 St Thomas' Street, Oxford OX1 1JG
by arrangement with Samuel French Ltd.

British Library Cataloguing in Publication Data

Sutherland, Dan
    Six miniatures, each for five ladies.
    I. Title
    822'.914   PR6069.U78/

Hardback ISBN 1-85089-189-3

Paperback ISBN 1-85089-199-0

Phototypeset, printed and bound by Unwin Brothers Limited, Old Woking, Surrey.

Cover designed by CGS Studios, Cheltenham.

PROGRAMME

MOTHERS KNOW BEST
(A Miniature Domestic Comedy)

CHARACTERS

Mrs Lolly Martin
Grannie
Mrs Margaret Parsons
Mavis
Freda

Scene. — A comfortable living-room in a country cottage.

Time. — One peaceful afternoon.

MOTHERS KNOW BEST

SCENE. — The living room of a country cottage. Afternoon.

    The room is comfortably furnished, in good taste. A window, back C., looks out on a cheerful garden. A door, up stage in the L. wall, leads to the hall. The fireplace is presumed to be in the fourth wall. Against the R. wall is a small writing table with a waste-paper basket under it. Down stage of this table is a small occasional table or a stand for a plant, and a pouffe. There is nothing on it. Above and L. of the writing table, a few paces away from it, is an armchair. Very slightly L. of C. is a small round table, with a runner. There is a wooden chair, with arms, slightly above and L. of the table. Down L. is another armchair. R. of the windows at the back is another occasional table, or plant stand, unoccupied. The upper L. corner of the room may be filled with a bookcase or corner cupboard.

(See the Ground Plan at the end of the Play.)

When the CURTAIN rises, MRS LOLLY MARTIN is standing above the table C., arranging flowers in a vase. She is about forty-five, and somewhat "arty" in dress and hair style. Seated in the armchair R., is her mother (GRANNIE), a very old lady in cap and shawl, rocking gently and reading a book. She is very deaf, but placid and content. Having finished the flowers, LOLLIE carries the vase, after some deliberation, to the stand down R., sets it, and retreats to judge the effect. Changing her mind, she carries the vase to the stand up R.C., by the window, and sets it again. This satisfies her, and she moves down to L. of GRANNIE'S chair.

LOLLY (*pointing to the vase up stage*). How do you like that?

(GRANNIE, *not hearing does not look up.*)

(*Louder.*) Grannie — how do you like that? (*She points up* R. *again.*)

GRANNIE (*turning a page, without looking up*). Eh?

LOLLY. Oh, never mind. (*She retreats a pace towards* C., *still looking at the vase.*)

(MRS MARGARET PARSONS *enters. She is about the same age as* LOLLY, *but much more of the "sensible" type. She is wearing outdoor clothes and carrying a shopping basket.*)

MARGARET (*moving to* L. *of the table*). Have the girls arrived yet? (*She puts the basket on the table.*)

LOLLY (*still staring at the vase*). Oh, hullo, Margaret. No, not yet.

MARGARET. Good — I was afraid I wouldn't be back in time. (*She takes off her hat and coat and subsides comfortably into the chair down* L.)

LOLLY. It wouldn't have mattered, would it? I mean, a few minutes? (*She drags her eyes from the vase, and turns.*)

MARGARET. If our daughters come all the way from London to see us, I think the least we can do is to be in when they arrive.

LOLLY. Yes, dear — of course. (*Pointing up* R.) Do you like the flowers in that corner — or down there? (*She points down* R.)

MARGARET (*nodding towards the little table down* R.). Down there, I think.

LOLLY (*disappointed*). Oh, do you? I like them where they are. Still, if you say so . . . (*She crosses up* R., *and takes the vase to down* R.)

MARGARET (*generously*). Put them where you like, Lolly — I don't mind.

4

LOLLY (*turning down* R.; *magnanimously*). No, dear — just as you like.

MARGARET. No, really ——

LOLLY (*cutting in; firmly*). Now, Margaret, when we took this place together we promised we'd never argue, didn't we? (*Moving up to the table.*) Did you get the biscuits?

MARGARET. Yes. They're in the basket.

(LOLLY *investigates the shopping basket.* MARGARET *relaxes comfortably in the chair.*)

You know, Lolly — we've an awful lot to be thankful for, haven't we? This nice little place of our own, our daughters happily married, no men to worry us ——

LOLLY. Only Grannie.

MARGARET (*affectionately*). Dear old thing — she's no trouble.

(*During this,* LOLLY *has found a biscuit and popped it into her mouth. She pulls a wry face.*)

LOLLY. Oh, dear!

MARGARET. What's the matter?

LOLLY. Caraway seed.

MARGARET (*anxiously*). Don't you like caraway seed?

LOLLY. I'm afraid not.

MARGARET (*concerned*). Oh, I *am* sorry. I simply adore them. So does Freda.

LOLLY (*heroically*). Never mind. (*Speaking on a sigh.*) Mavis and I can have bread and butter.

MARGARET (*starting to get up*). I'll go and get some others.

LOLLY (*restraining her with a gesture*). You will not! All the way up that hill to the village? I wouldn't hear of it.

You sit right there and have a cigarette. (*She takes the cigarette-box to* MARGARET.)

MARGARET (*allowing herself to be persuaded*). Oh, well . . .

(LOLLY *gives* MARGARET *a cigarette, takes one herself, lights them both. They puff in silence for a moment.* LOLLY *strolls up* C. *towards the window.*)

I showed you Freda's last letter, didn't I? Don't you think there was a faint hint of — well, something wrong between her and John?

LOLLY (*turning up* C.). As a matter of fact, Margaret, I did. I hesitated to say anything, of course, because after all she is *your* daughter and not mine. But . . . (*She shrugs her shoulders significantly and turns again to the window.*)

MARGARET. I thought Mavis's letter was a little strained, too.

LOLLY (*swinging round; very firmly*). Oh no, dear — oh, no! Mavis isn't the type to get upset over some trivial disagreement with her husband.

MARGARET. Nor is Freda, come to that.

LOLLY (*moving down to above the table; exasperatingly kind*). Not generally speaking, dear — no. But she *is* rather apt to put the emphasis on the wrong things, isn't she?

MARGARET (*a little coldly*). Is she?

LOLLY. Yes. Being a good cook and all that is very useful, of course. But we women have got to learn to handle *men*, as well as saucepans, haven't we? (*She smiles, condescendingly.*)

MARGARET (tartly). In the same way that you used to "handle" George when he was alive?

LOLLY (*changing instantly to asperity*). And what do you mean by that, Margaret?

MARGARET. Well, dear — let's face it — you and he used to have the most frightful rows, now didn't you?

LOLLY (*with dignity*). We had our differences, perhaps. Every married couple does. (*As she moves* L. *of the table to below the chair.*) I remember that holiday we all had together at Bournemouth, for instance — when you and Arthur wouldn't sit at the same table. Looked so silly, I thought, him having his meals off the mantlepiece. (*She sits.*)

MARGARET. He was just having one of his stubborn moods.

LOLLY (*adjusting her hair; casually*). Quite so. That's just it.

MARGARET (*irritated*). What do you mean — "Quite so that's just it"?

LOLLY. I'm afraid your Freda takes after him.

MARGARET (*sitting erect; curtly*). I don't think she does at all.

LOLLY (*with maddening tact*). I've no doubt you're the best one to judge, dear. But if she doesn't get it from him, where does she get it from?

MARGARET. Associating with your Mavis, perhaps.

LOLLY. Oh, come now! Stubborn is the last thing anyone could call Mavis.

MARGARET. What about the time she unscrewed the legs of the piano rather than practise her scales?

LOLLY (*with an airy gesture*). You must make allowances for the artistic temperament, Margaret.

MARGARET. I'd have made allowances with a big thick stick if she'd been my child. I brought up Freda very differently.

LOLLY. Yes — and now you see the result. Married only a year and her marriage is breaking up.

7

MARGARET. As a matter of fact, I don't think it's *Freda's* marriage that's breaking up. I think it's *Mavis's*.

LOLLY (*laughing*). Oh, nonsense. . . . (*She breaks off, and then continues uneasily.*) What do you mean?

MARGARET. Well, frankly, I've been expecting trouble from that quarter for a long time. Bringing up a child to play the piano and paint and that sort of thing is all very well, but husbands like to *eat*.

LOLLY (*rising*). Are you suggesting Mavis can't cook?

MARGARET. As far as I know, she can't boil a kettle of water.

LOLLY (*moving* R.C., *below the table; crossly*). Just because you've brought your daughter up to be a domestic drudge . . . (*She moves up stage.*)

MARGARET (*with spirit*). I've done no such thing! But at least I've taught her how to make a *home* ——

LOLLY (*turning, at up* R.C.). Yes —— and look what's happened to it!

MARGARET. Anyway, it had a better chance of success than Mavis's.

LOLLY (*trying to keep control*). Why, may I ask?

MARGARET. Because, to be quite honest with you, Lolly —— you hadn't the faintest idea how to bring up that child.

LOLLY (*easing a pace to* C.; *dangerously*). No?

MARGARET. No. (*Sitting back; with airy disdain.*) All this artistic nonsense. Spending hours on where to put the flowers. If she'd been taught how to run a *home*, her marriage might have had a chance. But she wasn't. She's as domesticated as Cleopatra's Needle —— and just about as useful.

LOLLY (*boiling*). Finished? Now you listen to me. (*She goes to the table and holds aloft the bag of biscuits; dramatically.*) That's you. *Caraway seeds!* Typical of you and the

8

way you've brought up Freda — completely without any understanding of the finer things of life.

MARGARET. Nonsense.

LOLLY. Nasty vulgar little black things that get stuck between your teeth. No wonder Freda's husband is leaving her!

MARGARET (*rising; exasperated*). Now look here, Lolly ——

LOLLY. I will *not* look there. The trouble with you is that you're narrow-minded, bigoted, prejudiced and uncultured ——

MARGARET (*going up* L.C., *level with* LOLLY). Oh, so that's what you think, is it?

LOLLY. Yes, it *is*. And if you ask Grannie here she'll say the same — won't you, Grannie? (*Turning to* GRANNIE.) *Grannie!*

GRANNIE (*turning her head a little*). Eh?

LOLLY. Oh, never mind.

(GRANNIE *resumes her reading, calmly.*)

MARGARET. If you think I'm going to stay in this house after that you're very much mistaken! For the first time in my life I understand what your late lamented husband meant when he said, "There's nothing wrong with Lolly that couldn't be put right by a good dose of arsenic." (*She marches to the door* L., *and turns there.*) And *how* I agree!

(*She exits triumphantly.* LOLLY *stares after her angrily for a moment, then takes the bag of caraway-seed biscuits and dumps it in the waste-paper basket. The vase of flowers catches her eye — she picks it up and carries it to its original place up* R., *with a bang.* GRANNIE *reads on,*

9

unnoticing. MAVIS *appears in the doorway. She is a pretty girl in her twenties, dressed in smart outdoor clothes.*)

MAVIS. Hullo, Mother.
LOLLY (*startled*). Mavis!

(*They move towards each other, meet at up* C., *and embrace.*)

You made me jump! Where did you spring from?
MAVIS. The door was open so I just walked in. Hullo, Gran.

(*She runs to* R. *and kisses* GRANNIE *lightly on the top of the head.* GRANNIE *flicks casually as at a fly, and doesn't look up.*)

LOLLY (*moving down* L.C.). Where's Freda?
MAVIS. She's putting the car away. (*Moving to down* R.C.) Well, darling — you look wonderful — how do I look?
LOLLY (*going to* MAVIS *and holding her at arm's length and looking at her searchingly*). Poor Mavis. . . . (*She breaks off and shakes her head.*)
MAVIS (*startled*). What's the matter?
LOLLY (*drawing her to* L.). Come over here and sit down and tell me *all* about it!

(MAVIS *sits in the chair down* L., *and* LOLLY *on the chair* L. *of the table.*)

MAVIS. There isn't much to tell, really.
LOLLY. What led up to it? Was it — was it trouble over cooking?
MAVIS (*amazed*). Good heavens, no! Why?
LOLLY. Your Aunt Margaret blames me for it. According to her, all this trouble between you and Frank is due to the way I brought you up ——

MAVIS. But there *isn't* any trouble!

LOLLY (*taken aback*). What? (*She rises.*) But your letter said ——

MAVIS (*rising; laughing*). Oh, Mother! (*She crosses* C., *to below the table, turns and sits on the edge of it.*) You've got it all wrong! We haven't quarrelled — in fact, we've never been happier.

LOLLY. But what — I don't . . . (*She breaks off bewildered.*)

MAVIS. I'm going to have a baby.

LOLLY (*moving to* MAVIS). What!

MAVIS (*composedly*). Yes.

LOLLY (*hugging her*). Oh, Mavis darling — how *wonderful!* I'm so glad for you. (*Earnestly.*) Are you *sure* you and Frank haven't quarrelled?

MAVIS (*laughing*). Quite sure.

LOLLY. And Frank hasn't said anything about your cooking or your housekeeping or anything like that?

MAVIS. Not a word.

(LOLLY *turns, moves up* L.C., *and stares grimly at the door* L.)

LOLLY. So! I don't know how to bring up a daughter, don't I? *Her* daughter's marriage is going on the rocks, whilst *my* daughter's — ha!

MAVIS (*surprised*). But, Mother . . . (*She breaks off, staring at* LOLLY.)

LOLLY (*ignoring her*). I'll tell her a thing or two! (*She goes to the door and calls with saccharine sweetness.*) Margaret! (*A pause.*) Oh, Margaret — come do-own! (*She turns from the door.*)

MAVIS. Mother — what's all this about Freda?

LOLLY (*easing to* L.C.). Well, dear — it's rather a long

story. I'll tell you later. (*Crossing impulsively to* MAVIS.) But you couldn't have brought me better news. Oh, darling — I'm so happy! (*She embraces* MAVIS.)

(MARGARET *enters.*)

MARGARET (*moving in to* L.C.). Hullo, Mavis. (*Coldly.*) You were calling, Lolly?

LOLLY (*dramatically; to* MAVIS). Tell her!

MAVIS (*moving up* L.C. *to* MARGARET; *laughing*). It's only that I'm going to have a baby, that's all.

LOLLY (*as she moves with triumphant gestures up stage,* R. *of the table*). And she has *not* quarrelled with Frank, they are *not* separating, and he does *not* complain about her cooking. (*She regards them from up* R.C.)

MARGARET. Oh. I — I'm glad to hear it. (*To* MAVIS.) Congratulations, dear.

MAVIS. Thank you.

(MARGARET *gives her a rather abstracted kiss.*)

MARGARET. Where's Freda?

MAVIS. She's outside, putting the car away. I'll go and tell her to buck up.

(*She exits.*)

LOLLY. Well, Margaret?

(MARGARET *does not answer. She moves up* C. *to the window.*)

(*Gently.*) You see, that old saying about the way to a man's heart being through his stomach — it may have been all right in the past, but today it's out of date. A man expects something more than a mere housekeeper. A woman must appeal to his intellect, his artistic sense. I don't want to be unkind, Margaret, but if you had brought up Freda in the same way that I brought up Mavis ——

(MAVIS *enters with* FREDA *in her wake.* FREDA *is a pretty girl of about* MAVIS'S *age, equally nicely dressed and equally cheerful and smiling.*)

MAVIS. Here she is.

FREDA (*running up stage to* MARGARET). Hullo, Mummy darling! . . .

MARGARET (*meeting her up* L.C.). Freda!

(MARGARET *and* FREDA *embrace.* MAVIS *moves down* L.)

LOLLY. Well, Freda?

FREDA. Hullo, Aunt Lolly! (*She moves to* LOLLY, *kisses her, and goes to above* GRANNIE'S *chair, kissing the top of her head.*) Hullo, Gran!

(GRANNIE *again brushes her head as if a fly were there.* FREDA *moves down* R.C. *and turns.*)

Well, I must say everyone's looking very well.

MARGARET (*searchingly*). And you, my dear — are you very worried?

FREDA (*surprised*). Me? (*As she moves up* C. *between* LOLLY *and* MARGARET.) No, I'm not worried. Anyway, it's ages yet.

MARGARET. What is?

FREDA (*to* MAVIS). Didn't you tell them?

MAVIS (*perching on the upper arm of the chair down* L.). I didn't get a chance.

MARGARET. Freda! You're not . . .?

FREDA. Yes, I am. December.

MARGARET (*unbelievingly*). A baby?

FREDA. Yes, of course. I gave you a pretty broad hint in my letter. Do you mean to say you didn't guess?

MARGARET (*immensely relieved*). Oh, Freda, darling!

(*She embraces* FREDA *warmly*.)

LOLLY (*a bit disconcerted*). Er — congratulations, Freda.

FREDA. Thank you.

(MARGARET *looks at* LOLLY *with a gleam in her eye*.)

MARGARET. Lolly, I think you and I have a few things to discuss.

MAVIS (*rising*). Well, whilst you're doing that, Freda and I will get the tea. Anything to eat?

MARGARET. Only some caraway-seed biscuits.

MAVIS. Oh, good — I simply adore them.

LOLLY (*in amazement*). Mavis! You don't!

MAVIS. I do — but you'd never let me have any.

FREDA. You can have mine — I loathe them. (*Crossing* L.) Come on, let's see what we can find.

(FREDA *and* MAVIS *exit*.)

LOLLY (*not looking at* MARGARET). They're in the waste-paper basket.

MARGARET. What are?

LOLLY. The Biscuits.

MARGARET. Oh. (*She crosses down* R., *fishes the biscuits out of the waste-paper basket, and then turns to go*.)

LOLLY. Margaret. . . . (*She moves down* C., *below the table*.)

MARGARET (*pausing*). Yes?

LOLLY (*turning*). I'm sorry I said all those things.

MARGARET. That's all right, Lolly.

LOLLY. You — you're not going, are you?

MARGARET. Not if you don't want me to.

LOLLY. Of course I don't.

(MARGARET *moves to her. They embrace.*)

MARGARET. I was just thinking — couldn't we turn the attic into a playroom?

LOLLY (*delightedly*). What a wonderful idea!

MARGARET. Then, when the babies came down here ——

LOLLY. We could keep an eye on the way they're being brought up ——

MARGARET. And see they're getting a proper domestic foundation ——

LOLLY. You mean, a proper artistic training ——

MARGARET (*warningly*). Now, Lolly!

LOLLY (*warningly*). Now, Margaret!

(*For a moment it looks as if they are going to start all over again. Then they laugh. An idea suddenly strikes* LOLLY.)

Grannie! We haven't told Grannie the news!

(*They both go over to* GRANNIE *and bellow in her ear,*
MARGARET R. *of her chair and* LOLLY L.)

LOLLY
MARGARET } (*together*). Grannie!

GRANNIE. Eh?

LOLLY (*shouting*). Mavis and Freda are going to have a baby.

GRANNIE. What — one between two of them?

MARGARET (*shouting*). No, no — one each.

GRANNIE. Are they married?

LOLLY. What? Yes, of course they are!

GRANNIE. Then what are you worrying about?

MARGARET. We're not worrying — we're delighted.

GRANNIE. Good. All I hope is that they make a better job of bringing *their* children up than you did in bringing *them* up. Proper mess you made of it — both of you. Why, neither of them has the least idea how to do a sampler. Now, you two girls sit down there, and listen to me for a moment.

(MARGARET *sits on the pouffe, down* R. *and* LOLLY *sits* L. *of the table, like unwilling children.*)

In my opinion, the whole theory of bringing up children, bringing them up properly, of course, comes down to half a dozen quite clearly defined points. . . .

As she talks, and the others listen with an air of resignation,

the CURTAIN *falls.*

FURNITURE AND PROPERTY PLOT

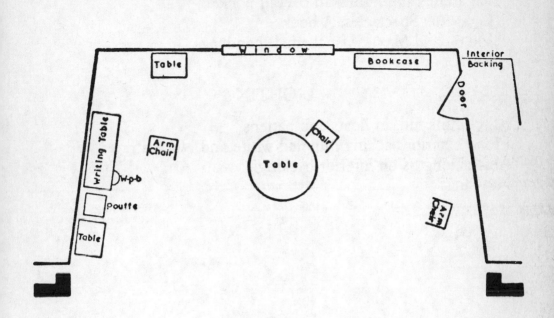

Carpet on stage. Chintz curtains at the windows.
Pictures: good water colours.
Small writing table. Usual dressings. UNDER IT: waste-paper basket.
1 small round table (L. OF C.).
2 occasional tables, or plant stands (DOWN R. AND UP R.).
1 wooden chair with arms (L. OF TABLE C.).
1 armchair R.C.
1 armchair down L.
1 pouffe (R. BELOW WRITING TABLE).
OTHER FURNITURE TO DRESS, AS DESIRED.

PROPERTIES:
    MARGARET: Shopping basket, filled with groceries, including a paper bag of biscuits.
    LOLLY (AT C. TABLE): "Arty" vase, with flowers.
    Cigarettes and lighter in overall pocket.
    GRANNIE: Spectacles. A book.
    FREDA and MAVIS: Usual small handbags.

LIGHTING

All circuits full, in floats and battens.
Flood exterior backing mingled white and No. 3 straw.
Amber lengths on interior backing.
NO CUES.

FOUR CHARACTERS AND A CORPSE
(A Miniature Murder Mystery)

CHARACTERS

Miss Farley
Molly Elton
Beatrice Landsdown
Elsie
The Corpse

Scene. — The Headmistress's study at St Bede's College.
Time. — One evening.

FOUR CHARACTERS AND A CORPSE

SCENE. — The Headmistress's study at St Bede's College.

It is a comfortable room, suitably furnished and cosy. There is a door at the back, C., a fireplace R., a large desk L.C., set up and down stage, with a large chair L. of it, and smaller ones R. and below it. Curtains at L. suggest the presence of windows. At R.C., a large armchair is turned to face up slightly R. The angle it makes is sufficient to reveal a woman's arm hanging limply over the side nearest the fire, and also the top of her head. The arm is stained ominously red. This half of the room is lighted mainly by the glow of the fire. On the desk is a shaded reading lamp, and a small shaded table lamp is on an occasional table down L. These light the L. half of the room, and shed a little towards R. But the armchair is in comparative shadow.

(See the Ground Plan at the end of the Play.)

When the CURTAIN rises, the Headmistress, MISS FARLEY, is standing above and L. of the armchair looking thoughtfully at the body in the chair. She is in her fifties, and has a strong, intelligent face. MOLLY ELTON enters up C. She is in her late twenties, attractive, and well dressed. As she enters, she turns a little towards MISS FARLEY, and pulls up in horror at what she sees.

MOLLY (*nearly screaming*). Oh!

MISS FARLEY (*turning; evenly*). Shut the door, Molly.

(MOLLY *does so, still staring in fascinated horror at the chair.*)

MOLLY. What's happened?

MISS FARLEY (*grimly*). Pretty obvious, isn't it?

MOLLY (*moving down; slowly*). Is — is she dead?

MISS FARLEY (*moving towards her*). I'm afraid so.

MOLLY (*breaking down*). Oh, poor Evelyn. . . . (*She sobs, covering her face with her hands.*)

MISS FARLEY (*taking her arm; gently*). Steady now, Molly — come and sit down — here, drink this ——

(*She takes her to the chair* R. *of the desk. Having seated* MOLLY, *she pours out a glass of water and gives it to her.* MOLLY *sips it and pulls herself together with an effort.*)

MOLLY. I'm sorry. (*She shivers.*) It — it gave me such a shock.

MISS FARLEY. It's my fault — I should have warned you. (*She takes the glass and puts it on the desk.*)

MOLLY. But how did it happen? Who did it?

MISS FARLEY (*above the desk*). I don't know — yet.

MOLLY. Why should anyone want to kill Evelyn? (*She gives the armchair a quick glance, and then away.*)

MISS FARLEY (*slowly*). I've got an idea it may be connected with all these thefts we've been having in the school lately.

MOLLY. Oh. . . . (*She breaks off, a little embarrassed.*)

MISS FARLEY. I didn't tell the police about those because of the scandal it would have made. (*She pauses a moment.*) But now I'm afraid I've got no choice. (*She sits,* L. *of the desk.*)

MOLLY (*hesitantly*). You — you don't think that — Evelyn was the thief?

MISS FARLEY. If she were, why should she be murdered?

MOLLY (*as before*). I don't know.

MISS FARLEY. More likely to be the other way round, isn't it?

22

MOLLY. You mean she caught someone at it and they killed her?

MISS FARLEY. Possibly.

MOLLY. Oh, how terrible — poor Evelyn. . . . (*She falters.*)

MISS FARLEY. I found this on the floor by the chair.

(*She picks up a small object from her blotting pad.*)

MOLLY. What is it?

MISS FARLEY (*holding it out towards* MOLLY). A hairpin — of a rather unusual type.

(MOLLY *examines it.*)

Do you know anyone who uses pins like that?

MOLLY (*reluctantly*). I — well . . . (*She breaks off, again very embarrassed.*)

MISS FARLEY. If you do, I advise you to tell me.

MOLLY. Beatrice Landsdown does, I believe.

(MISS FARLEY *looks at her in silence. Then she picks up the house phone on her desk.*)

MISS FARLEY (*into the phone*). Beatrice? This is Miss Farley. Will you come over to my study right away, please. Yes, immediately. Thank you. (*She rings off.*)

MOLLY (*rising*). It couldn't be Beatrice — it *couldn't* be.

(*She moves, agitated, down* L. *and turns.*)

MISS FARLEY. We mustn't jump to conclusions, Molly. There may be a perfectly simple explanation.

MOLLY. I know they didn't get on together, but I can't believe that she'd — do *this*.

MISS FARLEY. What do you mean, they didn't get on?

MOLLY (*sinking into the chair below the desk*). I shouldn't have said that.

MISS FARLEY. If it's true, there's no harm in saying it.

MOLLY. Well, ever since Evelyn was elected treasurer of the Sports Club in place of Beatrice, Beatrice has hated her.

MISS FARLEY. And what was Evelyn's attitude to that?

MOLLY. She just ignored it. Which made it all the worse.

(*There is a knock at the door.*)

MISS FARLEY. Come in.

(BEATRICE LANDSDOWN *enters. She is plain, middle-aged and severely dressed. Facing the desk, she does not at first see the armchair and its contents.*)

BEATRICE. You wanted me, Miss Farley?

MISS FARLEY. Yes, Beatrice — come in.

(BEATRICE *moves down* C., *glancing unconsciously to* R. *She sees the chair, and catches her breath, but does not otherwise lose her composure.*)

BEATRICE. What's happened?

MISS FARLEY. I'm afraid it's — murder.

(BEATRICE *moves towards the chair.* MISS FARLEY *checks her half rising.*)

(*Quickly.*) You'd better not go near her.

BEATRICE (*pausing* R. *of* C.). Why not?

MISS FARLEY. There may be clues — we mustn't disturb anything.

BEATRICE. But ——

MISS FARLEY (*sharply*). Please do as I say, Beatrice. And sit down — I want to ask you some questions.

BEATRICE. Questions? Hadn't they better be left to the police? (*She sits in the chair* R. *of the desk.*)

MISS FARLEY. The police have been sent for. I have no doubt they will ask all the questions they wish. But there are two mysteries here and they may or may not be connected. I want to find out.

MOLLY. What do you mean?

MISS FARLEY. In addition to this terrible business, there has been another theft — Evelyn's room has been broken into and the Sports Club money stolen.

MOLLY. (*sitting erect*). What!

BEATRICE. When did that happen?

MISS FARLEY. That's the mystery — it appears to have taken place at the same time as — this. (*She indicates the armchair at* R.)

BEATRICE. One person obviously did both.

MISS FARLEY. No — that's just it. It *couldn't* have been the same person.

MOLLY. How do you know?

MISS FARLEY. Because it so happens that I am able to place the time of both the theft and the murder to within a few minutes. And as far as I can see, they occurred simultaneously.

MOLLY. I still don't understand. . . .

(*She breaks off as* MISS FARLEY *rises.*)

MISS FARLEY. A few minutes before seven I phoned Evelyn to come to my study about some exam papers. And certainly neither the robbery nor the murder had occurred then. Immediately after I'd phoned her I was called down to the Common Room.

BEATRICE. Leaving this room empty?

MISS FARLEY. No. The housemaid, Elsie, was here. (*As*

she moves slowly up C.) Some bits of leaves and things had blown in through the window and I'd sent for her to run the vacuum over the carpet. (*She turns to them, at* C.)

MOLLY. Then what happened?

MISS FARLEY. When I came upstairs again — exactly ten minutes later — I passed Evelyn's room. It was in complete chaos, with a broken cashbox lying in the middle of the floor, empty. Then I came here and found — this. (*She indicates the armchair.*)

(BEATRICE *and* MOLLY *look across at* EVELYN, *and then away.*)

MOLLY (*after a slight pause*). Couldn't one person have done both things?

MISS FARLEY. Impossible. The room was turned so completely upside down that whoever did it couldn't possibly have had time to come along here and do this also.

BEATRICE. And you left Elsie here in this room?

MISS FARLEY. Yes.

BEATRICE. Perhaps she can throw some light on it.

MISS FARLEY (*easing* R.C.). That's what I intend to find out. Molly — would you call down the stairs for her? The bell is out of order.

MOLLY (*rising*). Yes, of course. (*She moves* C., *to turn up to the door.*)

MISS FARLEY (*sharply*). Keep away from this chair.

(MOLLY *gives it a horrified look, keeps well clear of it, and exits.*)

BEATRICE. What was *she* doing here?

MISS FARLEY (*moving to the fire*). I sent for her — she was a particular friend of Evelyn's. (*She attends to the fire.*)

BEATRICE. Yes?

(MISS FARLEY *straightens up, and turns.*)

MISS FARLEY (*keenly*). You say that as though you don't believe they were.

BEATRICE. Frankly, I don't.

(MISS FARLEY *puts down the poker, and eases to* R.C.)

MISS FARLEY. Why not?

BEATRICE. I know that type — thick as thieves one minute and mortal enemies the next. There was more than a little jealousy there, you know.

MISS FARLEY. On whose side?

BEATRICE. Molly's.

MISS FARLEY. About what?

BEATRICE. (*shrugging*). I've no idea — but you could just *see* there was.

MISS FARLEY (*thoughtfully*). Mm. (*As she crosses to* L., *below the desk.*) I always understood they got on very well together.

BEATRICE. Naturally — that's what they wanted you to think.

MISS FARLEY (*turning up to her chair,* L., *of the desk*). They are of a different generation from ours, Beatrice — perhaps we don't understand them very well. (*She sits.*)

BEATRICE (*grimly*). *I* understand them well enough — empty-headed minxes thinking of nothing but clothes and painting their faces.

(*There is a knock at the door.*)

MISS FARLEY. Come in!

(*The door opens, and* MOLLY *enters, shepherding* ELSIE, *a pasty-faced young servant, who stares fearfully at the armchair and its occupant.*)

Shut the door.

(MOLLY *obeys, and moves to up* L.)

Elsie — you know what's happened, don't you?

ELSIE (*moving down a little, at* C.; *frightened*). Yes, m'm. Miss Elton has just told me.

MISS FARLEY. Well, come away from that chair — I want to ask you some questions.

ELSIE (*easing a pace towards the desk; tearfully*). I don't know anything about it, m'm — honest I don't. (*She is now standing below and* R. *of* BEATRICE'S *chair.*)

MISS FARLEY. Were you in here when Miss Evelyn arrived?

ELSIE. Yes, m'm — she got here just as I was going.

MISS FARLEY (*leaning forward*). Did you notice what time that was?

ELSIE. It was striking seven.

MISS FARLEY (*triumphantly*). Just as I thought! (*She sits back.*) It narrows down the time for both crimes to nine or ten minutes.

BEATRICE. I really don't see where all this is leading. . .

MISS FARLEY (*cutting in*). This part of the building, as you all know, is separate from all the rest — and there is only one way into it — through the Common Room.

BEATRICE. Well?

MISS FARLEY (*leaning forward*). All during those vital ten minutes I was standing in the doorway leading to the Common Room. Nobody could have come into or gone out of this part of the building without being seen by me.

BEATRICE. There are the windows.

MISS FARLEY. They all overlook the quadrangle — anyone trying to get in or out that way would have been seen by scores of people.

BEATRICE. I still don't see the trend of all this. . . .

MISS FARLEY (*interrupting her*). Besides Evelyn, there were only four people in this wing — and of those four one must have committed the robbery and one must have committed the murder.

BEATRICE (*half rising; indignantly*). Are you suggesting that I ——

MISS FARLEY (*interrupting*). I'm not suggesting anything ——

(BEATRICE *sits*.)

I'm merely pointing out the obvious facts. We four are the only possible suspects. Let us try a little elimination. Elsie — where did you go after you left this room?

ELSIE (*startled*). What, me? (*As she crosses quickly to above the desk in agitation*.) I didn't go anywhere — I didn't do anything — honest I didn't ——

MISS FARLEY. Don't be absurd — you must have gone somewhere.

ELSIE (*starting to cry*). All I did was lean out of the window at the end of the corridor and talk to Roberts, the porter — there wasn't no harm in that, was there?

MISS FARLEY. How long were you talking to him?

ELSIE. Till I heard you coming upstairs.

MISS FARLEY. So that accounts for you during that ten minutes.

BEATRICE. You've only her word for it.

ELSIE (*retreating a pace; indignantly*). Ooh, I . . .

(Miss Farley *checks her with a gesture and picks up the house phone.*)

Miss Farley (*into the phone*). Roberts? This is Miss Farley. When did you last see Elsie? (*A pause.*) How long were you talking? ... And she never left the window during the whole of that time? ... All right, Roberts, thank you. (*She hangs up the receiver and sits back.*) Well, Elsie, that's your alibi confirmed. Good. Just sit up there, my dear.

(Elsie *sits in the chair at the back wall.*)

Next, myself. Would anyone like to check that I was, in fact, standing in the doorway of the Common Room in full view of a couple of dozen people? Or do you accept that I would hardly be so stupid as to make up a story that could so easily be disproved?

(*Nobody answers.*)

Very well. That leaves only you two. Where were you, Molly?

Molly. I was in my room, reading.

Beatrice (*sneering*). That's very easily said.

Miss Farley (*rising*). All right, Beatrice — leave this to me, if you please. (*She crosses, slowly above the desk, to* c.)

Beatrice (*while* Miss Farley *crosses*). I don't see why we should have to put up with all this ——

Miss Farley (*interrupting*). I'll come to you in a moment. (*She looks across at* Molly.) Molly — can you *prove* that you were in your room during that ten minutes?

Molly (*alarmed*). No — I — I can't.

Miss Farley. And what about you, Beatrice?

Beatrice. I was in *my* room.

MISS FARLEY. Can you prove that?

BEATRICE (*without looking at her; haughtily*). You have my word for it.

MISS FARLEY (*regretfully*). I'm afraid, Beatrice, where murder is concerned, that isn't enough.

BEATRICE (*alarmed*). Murder? (*She turns in her chair.*) But I — you — you don't mean to suggest that I —— (*She rises.*) How dare you say such a thing!

MISS FARLEY. If I don't, the police will.

BEATRICE. The police!

MISS FARLEY. They're bound to ask the same questions, you know. Of both of you.

MOLLY (*gripping the arms of her chair; wildly*). But — but — you can't believe that *I* had anything to do with these things?

MISS FARLEY. My dear Molly, look at the facts. Two crimes have been committed and only two people could have done them — you and Beatrice. The only question is, who did which? And that, I grant you, is a pretty important question. The difference between a paltry theft of a few pounds and murder. . . .

BEATRICE (*moving round above and* R. *of her chair; very agitated*). I won't listen to this another moment — I won't — I won't ——

MISS FARLEY. Did you steal the money, Beatrice?

BEATRICE. No!

MISS FARLEY. Then in that case, you must have come into this room and ——

BEATRICE (*wildly*). No! I didn't — I didn't!

MISS FARLEY. Then will you explain how this came to be here? (*She holds out the hairpin*). One of your hairpins. It was found in this room.

BEATRICE (*bluffing it out, but frightened*). Well, what of

it? I come in here often enough. I could have dropped it yesterday, this morning, any time. . . . (*She falters.*)

MISS FARLEY (*steadily*). No — not *any* time. It must have been dropped *after* Elsie vacuumed the carpet. In other words, between seven and ten-past.

BEATRICE (*now thoroughly frightened*). What are you saying?

MISS FARLEY. You were in this room, Beatrice ——

BEATRICE (*desperately*). I wasn't — I wasn't! I swear I wasn't!

MISS FARLEY. What about this pin?

BEATRICE. I don't know how it got there — but I didn't kill her — I didn't, I *didn't*! (*She stares at* MISS FARLEY.)

MISS FARLEY (*gently*). I'm afraid, Beatrice, all the evidence suggests that you did.

BEATRICE (*panicking*). No! No — you mustn't say that — I didn't do it — I didn't!

MISS FARLEY. And there is only your unsupported word to the contrary.

BEATRICE (*desperately*). No — no — I can prove it!

MISS FARLEY. How?

BEATRICE (*after a pause*). Because — I took the money.

(*There is a silence.*)

MISS FARLEY (*quietly*). You took the money?

BEATRICE (*moving to* L. *of* MISS FARLEY *at* C.). Yes — yes — I took it! That proves I *couldn't* have killed her, doesn't it? You said so yourself. I took it. You'll find it upstairs — in my trunk — every penny of it. (*Her voice rises hysterically as she turns, pointing to* MOLLY.) *I* didn't kill Evelyn — *she* did.

(MOLLY *springs to her feet.*)

MISS FARLEY. I don't think she did, Beatrice. In fact, I *know* she didn't.

BEATRICE. What! But you said . . .

MISS FARLEY (*cutting in*). One moment. (*She turns to the chair.*) Evelyn.

(*The "corpse" rises, revealing herself as an attractive young woman, uninjured, but her blouse heavily stained with red. ELSIE utters a yelp of fright, and breaks below and L. of the doorway.*)

EVELYN. Yes, Miss Farley?

MOLLY (*astounded*). *Evelyn!* (*Overcome with emotion, she runs across to* EVELYN.) Oh, *Evelyn!* Then you — you — you . . . (*She hugs* EVELYN, *half laughing, half crying.*)

EVELYN. Hey! Bear up! (*She sits on the* L. *arm of the armchair and puts her arm round* MOLLY.)

(BEATRICE *has been gaping at* EVELYN. *She now turns furiously on* MISS FARLEY.)

BEATRICE. What does this mean?

MISS FARLEY. It means, Beatrice, that I've been suspecting you of these thefts for a long time. The only way to get you to confess was to face you with a worse alternative — a charge of murder.

BEATRICE (*retreating below the chair* R. *of the desk; almost incoherent*). Why, you — you . (*She is now pressed against the* R. *edge of the desk, gazing venomously at* MISS FARLEY.)

MISS FARLEY (*unruffled*). So with a quite convincing corpse — if you didn't get too near her — and a planted hairpin, we managed it, didn't we?

BEATRICE. You don't imagine you're going to get away with it, do you?

MISS FARLEY (*mildly*). Oh yes, Beatrice — oh, yes, I do.

And I'm quite sure that you're going to pack your things and get out of here within an hour — leaving, of course, the money in your room. Or shall I *really* send for the police?

(*For a moment* BEATRICE *still glares, her hands working with rage. Then, suddenly, without a word, she marches up to the door, thrusting* ELSIE *aside, and exits.*)

What a *very* unpleasant person she is. (*Patting* MOLLY'S *shoulder.*) I'm sorry I had to put you through this. I must make it up to you, my dear, somehow. And I must buy *you* a new blouse, Evelyn. (*She turns to* ELSIE.) Now make a nice, strong pot of tea, Elsie, my dear, and have one yourself.

(ELSIE *smiles wanly, and goes to the door.*)

I must think of a treat for you — Oh, and Elsie . . . you might fill my red ink bottle — it's empty.

She smiles kindly at ELSIE *as she goes, and then turns to the others as —*

the CURTAIN *falls*

FURNITURE AND PROPERTY PLOT

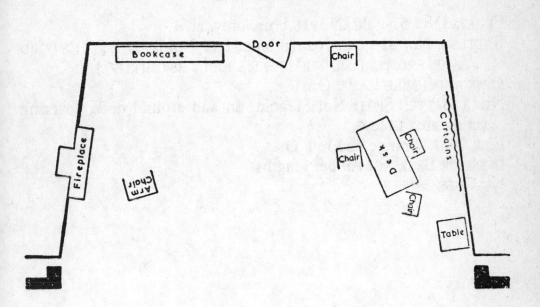

Carpet on stage. Rug at hearth. Thick curtains at window.

ON THE WALLS: one or two good reproductions. Also photographs of groups of students, hockey teams, etc.

1 large armchair (R.C.).

1 large table desk. ON IT: shaded reading lamp, blotting pad, inkstand, a book or two, house phone, carafe of water and glass.

1 large wooden chair, with arms (L. OF DESK).

1 smaller chair, with arms (BELOW LOWER END OF DESK).

1 bookcase (BACK R.C.).

1 Chair against back wall (UP L.C.).

1 occasional table (or card index filing unit))DOWN L. BELOW WINDOW). ON IT: shaded lamp.

Fender, fire-irons, coal scuttle (AT FIREPLACE).

PERSONAL:
MISS FARLEY: 1 hairpin of unusual type.

LIGHTING

FLOATS: No. 51 gold, No. 18 blue, only, at ¼.

BATTENS: No. 51 gold, No. 18 blue, No. 7 pink, at ½. (THE GOLD IN LAMPS FROM C. TO R. IN BATTENS, SHOULD BE OMITTED.)

DESK AND TABLE LAMP: On.

NO. 1 BATTEN SPOT: No. 51 gold, on and around desk, covering acting area L. to C.

FIRE SPOT: Orange and red. ON.

INTERIOR BACKING: Amber lengths.

NO CUES.

MIXING WITH THE RIGHT PEOPLE
(A Miniature Farce)

CHARACTERS

PAULINE
FELICITY
AUNT STELLA
MRS MOGGS
MRS BULLOCK

SCENE.—The lounge in AUNT STELLA'S house in the country.
TIME.—One summer afternoon.

MIXING WITH THE RIGHT PEOPLE

SCENE.—The lounge of AUNT STELLA'S house in the country. A summer afternoon.

There are french windows at the back C., a door up stage L., a settee at R., set at an angle, with an occasional table L. of it. Above the table is a chair. Another occasional table stands down R. An armchair stands down L. Below it is a small table with a telephone on it. The room is not over-crowded, but other furniture may be added as desired by the producer.

(See the Ground Plan at the end of the Play.)

When the CURTAIN rises, PAULINE and her cousin FELICITY, two pretty young women, are seated, PAULINE on the settee and FELICITY at L., scanning magazines. They are lolling in negligent attitudes and appear to be bored. They wear charming garden party frocks.

PAULINE (*stretching and yawning*). Oh lord — isn't this dreary Sale of Work ever going to start?

FELICITY. It will as soon as Mrs What's-her-name gets here.

PAULINE. What *is* her name, by the way?

FELICITY. I don't know anything about her except that she's the wife of the new M.P. and that Aunt Stella has written her gushing letters asking her to open this footling nonsense out in the garden.

PAULINE. You know, if Aunt Stella ever gets to heaven I expect she'll immediately organize a Sale of Work and persuade the Archangel Gabriel to open it.

(*They laugh, but break off as* AUNT STELLA *enters up* L. *She is a bustling, busy type of woman, elegantly dressed for the Garden Fete.*)

AUNT STELLA (*moving to* C.). Now, what are you girls doing in here?

PAULINE. We're waiting for Mrs What's-her-name to arrive, Aunt Stella.

AUNT STELLA. Well, she's not likely to arrive down the chimney, is she? (*Taking the flowers from the table* R.C. *to the side table* L.) You ought to be out waiting for her at the gates.

FELICITY (*meekly*). Yes, Aunt Stella.

AUNT STELLA (*bustling about the room, adjusting this and that*). And don't call her Mrs What's-her-name — it isn't respectful.

PAULINE. We don't know her real name.

AUNT STELLA (*moving to above the* L. *end of the settee*). It's Mrs Bullock.

PAULINE. Oh well — if it is, it is.

AUNT STELLA (*severely*). And what, pray, do you mean by that absurd remark?

PAULINE (*meekly*). Nothing, Aunt Stella.

AUNT STELLA. Then why make it? (*Clapping her hands and gesticulating.*) Come on, now — outside, both of you, and keep watch for her.

FELICITY (*rising lazily*). What does she look like?

(*As* AUNT STELLA *replies,* PAULINE *sits up slowly and adjusts her hair.*)

AUNT STELLA. Not having had the honour of meeting her yet, I'm unable to say. But obviously a person of bearing and distinction.

FELICITY. A prize Bullock, in fact.

AUNT STELLA. Felicity, that is neither funny nor in good taste.

FELICITY (*meekly*). No, Aunt Stella.

AUNT STELLA. You girls have no sense of social import-ance. Nor of the value of mixing with the right people. Mrs Bullock has paid us a great compliment by promising to come here and we must treat her accordingly.

PAULINE }
FELICITY } (*meekly*). Yes, Aunt Stella.

AUNT STELLA. Very well, then. See that you remember it.

(*After giving them a stern look*, AUNT STELLA *turns up and sweeps out through the french windows.*)

PAULINE. Well, of all the copper-bottomed, brass-bound snobs!

FELICITY. Serve her right if Mrs What's-her-name didn't turn up.

PAULINE. She wouldn't dare.

(*There is a knock at the door.*)

Come in.

(MRS MOGGS *enters, and crosses to* C. *She is a charwoman of uncertain age and indefinite shape. She wears a man's cloth cap, shabby clothes, and a coarse apron. She carries a bucket and mop.*)

MRS MOGGS. Ow, excuse me ——

FELICITY (*breaking in; hopefully*). You're not Mrs What's-her-name, by any chance?

MRS MOGGS. No, I'm Mrs Moggs — the new charlady.

FELICITY. Oh. Pity. (*She sits on the arm of her chair.*)

MRS MOGGS. I've come to do the cleaning after this 'ere Sale of Work.

PAULINE. I'm afraid you're a bit early — it hasn't started yet.

MRS MOGGS. No, but I come early because of my old man, you see. 'E's bin took on, too.

PAULINE. Took on too?

MRS MOGGS. That's right. As a waiter. Just for the afternoon, like. But I've lorst 'im — can't find 'im nowhere.

FELICITY. Have you tried the tea tent?

MRS MOGGS. Ow, yes. And the ice-cream stall. But 'e ain't there.

PAULINE. Perhaps he's in the kitchen — it's down the corridor on the left.

MRS MOGGS. I 'ope so. Because if 'e ain't, it means 'e's gorn to sleep again.

FELICITY. Gone to sleep?

MRS MOGGS. Always doing it, 'e is. Leave 'im alone for five minutes and — bang! — 'e's asleep.

FELICITY (*gravely*). Well, if we find him, we'll wake him up for you.

MRS MOGGS. Thank you, miss. And if you 'ave any difficulty, just kick 'im in the stummick — not 'ard, you understand, but firmly. It's the only thing that does it.

FELICITY. We'll keep it in mind.

MRS MOGGS (*starting to move* L.). Thank you, miss. (*She checks at* L.C.) Where did you say the kitchen was?

PAULINE. Down the corridor on the left.

MRS MOGGS. Ow, thank you.

(*She exits. The girls giggle.*)

FELICITY (*rising and easing to* C.). Can you imagine what their honeymoon must have been like?

PAULINE. A series of dull thuds, I should think.

(*The phone rings.* FELICITY *crosses down* L. *and answers it.*)

FELICITY (*into the phone*). Mrs Pobsleigh's house . . . No, this is her niece speaking. (*A pause.*) Oh. . . . Oh, I see — yes, I'll tell her — good-bye. (*She rings off, and turns to* PAULINE *delightedly.*) Mrs What's-her-name can't get here. Her car's broken down.

PAULINE. Aunt Stella will be pleased!

FELICITY (*as she moves to* C.; *regretfully*). And I was so looking forward to asking Mrs Bullock about all the little heifers.

PAULINE. Doesn't look as if we're going to mix with the right people after all. Come on, we'd better break the news to Aunt Stella.

(FELICITY *looks at the door* L., *pauses, and turns to* PAULINE.)

FELICITY. Pauline — I've just had a wonderful idea!

PAULINE (*catching on immediately*). Not — (*rising*) — Mrs Moggs?

FELICITY. Yes.

PAULINE. Do you think we could get away with it?

FELICITY. Why not? Nobody here knows either of them. And nobody except us knows that Mrs What's-her-name isn't coming.

PAULINE (*thoughtfully*). It's an idea.

(*There is a knock at the door.* MRS MOGGS *enters.*)

MRS MOGGS (*crossing to* L.C.; *worried*). 'E ain't in the kitchen ——

FELICITY (*cutting in*). Oh, Mrs Moggs — we were just talking about you. You haven't met my aunt yet, have you?

MRS MOGGS. 'Aven't met no-one.

FELICITY. Good. I mean — er — I think you should. She's very interested in cases like your husband's.

MRS MOGGS (*surprised*). Is she?

PAULINE. Oh, yes! Spent years studying them in — er — Central Africa. It's an epidemic disease of the pygmies, you know.

MRS MOGGS. I didn't know 'e 'ad anything wrong with 'is pygmies.

FELICITY. She'd love to talk to you about it.

MRS MOGGS. Well, I don't mind, I'm sure. But I'm not exactly dressed for 'igh society, am I?

FELICITY. Don't let that worry you — my sister will soon find you some clothes.

PAULINE. Yes, of course. (*As she crosses to* MRS MOGGS.) Just come along with me, Mrs Moggs.

FELICITY. There's just one thing I ought to warn you about. My aunt never gets people's names right — she's bound to call you Mrs Elephant, or Mrs Antelope, or Mrs Bullock or something. It's a habit she got in Central Africa.

MRS MOGGS. Oh, well — we all 'ave our weaknesses, don't we?

(*She exits, followed by* PAULINE, *who gives a conspiratorial grin and a thumbs up to* FELICITY *as she goes.* FELICITY *goes up to the window and calls.*)

FELICITY. Aunt Stella. Aunt Stel-la.

(*She beckons. Then apparently satisfied that* AUNT STELLA *is on her way in, she turns back into the room. She sees*

44

MRS MOGG'S *bucket and mop and hastily hides them behind the settee and crosses* L. AUNT STELLA *enters.*)

AUNT STELLA. Really, Felicity — I do wish you wouldn't call out in that vulgar manner. What will Mrs Bullock think?

FELICITY (*down* L.C.). She's here.

AUNT STELLA (*surprised*). What? Who's here?

FELICITY. Mrs Bullock. Apparently she got lost and came in through the back door.

AUNT STELLA (*worried*). Oh, dear — what a bad start. Where is she now?

FELICITY. Upstairs with Pauline.

AUNT STELLA (*moving towards the door* L.). I must go and see if there is anything I can do ——

FELICITY (*quickly*). I wouldn't, if I were you. She's a bit upset.

AUNT STELLA. Oh, what's the matter?

FELICITY (*making up an excuse*). Well, apparently — er — er — she's lost her dog — and she's very devoted to it.

AUNT STELLA. Oh, how sad!

FELICITY. I think perhaps she would appreciate a few words of sympathy.

AUNT STELLA. Yes, of course. Very thoughtful of you, Felicity.

FELICITY. Sh! Here they come. . . .

(PAULINE *enters with* MRS MOGGS, *the latter very elegantly got up in a large picture hat and a feather boa and gaudy parasol.*)

PAULINE (*coming* L.C.; *to* MRS MOGGS). This is my Aunt Stella ——

MRS MOGGS (*moving* C.). Wotcher. (*She gives* AUNT STELLA *a nod*.)

AUNT STELLA. So nice of you to come, Mrs Bullock. (*She extends her hand*.)

MRS MOGGS (*shaking hands*). Moggs.

AUNT STELLA (*politely*). What did you say?

MRS MOGGS. I said "Moggs" — but don't let it worry you.

AUNT STELLA (*indicating the settee*). Do sit down.

(MRS MOGGS *crosses and sits on the settee.* AUNT STELLA *sits.* L. *of the table*.)

Would you care for a little refreshment before you start the afternoon's labours?

MRS MOGGS. I could do with a drop of Rosy.

AUNT STELLA. Rosy?

MRS MOGGS. Rosy Lee. Tea.

AUNT STELLA (*with a rather forced laugh*). Oh, yes — of course. Pauline dear — would you mind?

PAULINE. Not at all.

(*She exits, grinning at* FELICITY, *who sits in the armchair* L.)

AUNT STELLA. Now, Mrs Bullock. . . .

MRS MOGGS. Moggs.

AUNT STELLA. What?

MRS MOGGS. Moggs.

AUNT STELLA (*giving her a bewildered look, but passing it over*). Yes, quite. My niece was just telling me you've mislaid your little man. Where did you lose him?

MRS MOGGS. 'Ere somewhere. I expect 'e's gorn to sleep under a tree.

46

AUNT STELLA (*brightly*). Well, we'll soon have a search party out. Can you describe him?

MRS MOGGS (*thoughtfully*). Well, 'e's rather round-shouldered . . .

AUNT STELLA (*astonished*). Round-shouldered?

MRS MOGGS. Yes — it's through spending so much time in the garden, you know — digging.

AUNT STELLA. Ah, yes — bones, I suppose. The little rascal!

MRS MOGGS (*continuing the description, after a look of surprise*). Not much 'air, I'm afraid ——

AUNT STELLA (*cutting in; very interested*). Clipped — French style?

MRS MOGGS. No — pudding basin, English style.

AUNT STELLA. Ah, yes. How big was he?

MRS MOGGS. About five foot six ——

AUNT STELLA. What?

FELICITY (*interposing hastily*). That's when he's on his hind legs, I suppose?

MRS MOGGS. That's right — always on 'is 'ind legs about something or other.

AUNT STELLA (*completely at a loss*). How interesting. What colour was his coat?

MRS MOGGS. Oh, just an old brown one. And blue trousers.

AUNT STELLA. Trousers? Did you say trousers?

MRS MOGGS. Well, you'd 'ardly expect 'im to go around without any, would you?

(PAULINE *enters with the tea tray*.)

AUNT STELLA (*relieved*). Oh, thank you, Pauline.

(PAULINE *puts the tray down on the table*.)

Do you take sugar, Mrs Bullock?
  MRS MOGGS. Moggs. Yes, please.

(PAULINE *beckons* FELICITY, *who rises, and moves out of earshot of the others. They talk in undertones during the ensuing dialogue as* AUNT STELLA *pours the tea*.)

PAULINE (*moving* L.C.). She's here!
FELICITY (*moving* L.). Who is?
PAULINE. The real Mrs Bullock — got a lift on a milkcart.
FELICITY. Oh lord! Now what do we do?
PAULINE. Get rid of this character, for a start.

(*She makes a gesture indicating that she has an idea, approaches the table, and addresses* MRS MOGGS.)

Excuse me — I think I've found him for you. Fast asleep as you said.
  MRS MOGGS (*rising*). Ow, good. Where was 'e?
  PAULINE. Er — behind the hoopla tent.
  MRS MOGGS (*scornfully*). 'Oopla! At 'is age! (*She crosses towards* L.)
  AUNT STELLA. Shall I go and fetch him for you?
  MRS MOGGS (*checking and turning at* L.C.). No thanks — I'd better attend to 'im meself. I know 'is little tricks, you see.

(*She exits, followed by* PAULINE.).

AUNT STELLA. What an extraordinary woman!
FELICITY (*sitting in the armchair* L.). Very refreshing, I thought.
AUNT STELLA. But all that about a dog with trousers! Do you think she was serious?

48

FELICITY. I'm sure she was.

AUNT STELLA. But blue trousers!

FELICITY. I don't see that it makes any difference what colour they are.

(MRS BULLOCK *peers round the door. She is a rather shabby little woman in an out-of-date hat.*)

MRS BULLOCK. Excuse me — I'm looking for Mrs Pobsleigh.

AUNT STELLA. Oh, you're the woman to do the cleaning, I suppose? (*Pointing* L.) The kitchen's down the corridor on the left.

MRS BULLOCK. The kitchen? (*She moves in, to* L.C.) But I'm looking for ——

AUNT STELLA (*testily*). Now don't bother me now, my good woman. Down the corridor and on the left. (*She picks up her cup.*)

MRS BULLOCK (*with a pace to* C.). Yes, but look here ——

AUNT STELLA (*irritably*). Oh, for heaven's sake! Can't you see I'm busy? Go away. (*She sips her tea.*)

MRS BULLOCK (*hurt*). Well, that's a fine thing, I must say. Come all this way in a milkcart ——

AUNT STELLA (*cutting in, as she puts down her cup*). Now, I really can't be bothered with your troubles — I've got enough of my own.

MRS BULLOCK (*indignantly*). The least I expected was a cup of tea and a little politeness ——

AUNT STELLA (*rising*). Tea, indeed! When you've done your job you'll get your half-crown — and that's all. Now go away.

MRS BULLOCK (*her temper beginning to rise*). I've never been so insulted in all my life!

AUNT STELLA. The trouble with you people is that you've got ideas above your station.

MRS BULLOCK (*angrily*). Oh we have, have we!

AUNT STELLA. Yes, you have. A person like you . . .

MRS BULLOCK. Don't you call me a person!

AUNT STELLA. I shall call you whatever I like.

MRS BULLOCK (*loudly*). Oh no, you won't.

AUNT STELLA (*more loudly*). Oh yes, I will.

MRS BULLOCK (*shouting*). Now you listen to me . . .

AUNT STELLA (*also shouting*). I refuse to do anything of the kind.

(*While this is going on,* MRS MOGGS *appears in the doorway.* PAULINE *hovers anxiously in the background.*)

MRS MOGGS (*cutting in on the last phrase; in astonishment*). Ethel! (*She hurries to* C.)

(MRS BULLOCK *swings round in surprise.*)

MRS BULLOCK. Gertrude!

(*They embrace.* PAULINE *moves down* L. *to* FELICITY. AUNT STELLA *looks on in astonishment.*)

Fancy seeing you!

MRS MOGGS. What are you doing 'ere?

MRS BULLOCK. I'm supposed to be opening this bloomin' Sale of Work ——

AUNT STELLA. What!

MRS BULLOCK (*turning on her*). Of course! What d'you think I come all this way for?

AUNT STELLA. But — but — (*she tries to find words*) — are you Mrs Bullock?

MRS BULLOCK. Of course I am.

AUNT STELLA (*to* MRS MOGGS). Then who are you?

MRS MOGGS. I told you a dozen times — Moggs. Mrs Moggs — I've come to do the cleaning.

(AUNT STELLA *totters to her chair, her hand to her head.* MRS BULLOCK *and* MRS MOGGS *regard her with distaste.*)

AUNT STELLA. Oh, good heavens!

MRS BULLOCK (*turning to* MRS MOGGS). What's the matter with her?

MRS MOGGS. Barmy, I think. Kept suggesting my old man go round without 'is trousis.

MRS BULLOCK (*shocked*). Good gracious! Never think it to look at her, would you?

MRS MOGGS. Just shows you can't be too careful about the people you mix with.

MRS BULLOCK. You're quite right, dear. Come on — let's get out of this place and have a nice cup of Rosy Lee somewhere.

(*Arm in arm, and talking as they go, they move towards the door.*)

MRS MOGGS. 'Aven't seen you for years, dear — not since your old man took up politics. . . .

(AUNT STELLA *rising, makes a desperate effort to save the situation.*)

AUNT STELLA. Dear Mrs Bullock — please don't go. . . . I can explain everything.

MRS BULLOCK (*moving on; ignoring her*). Well, the point was, you see, he thought it would be easier than navvying. But I'm not so sure.

(*Still talking, they exit.*)

AUNT STELLA. Mrs Bullock — Mrs Bullock — look, here's some Rosy Lee. . . . Do stay and have some. . . .

(*She picks up the tray and hurries off after them.* PAULINE *and* FELICITY *look at each other and grin.*)

FELICITY (*solemnly*). Let that be a warning to you, Pauline. (*As she moves* R.) If you must mix with the right people ——

(*There is a crash of breaking crockery off.* FELICITY *pulls up short*, at R.C.)

PAULINE (*wincing*). — don't do it with a tea tray in your hand!

PAULINE *collapses into the armchair* L., *and* FELICITY *on to the settee, giggling. They bury themselves in their magazines, still laughing unrestrainedly, as* —

the CURTAIN *falls.*

FURNITURE AND PROPERTY PLOT

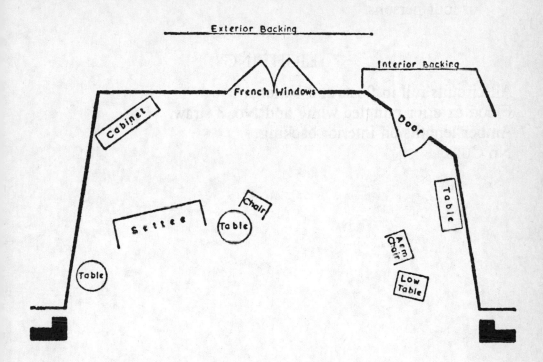

Carpet on stage. Light curtains at the french windows.
1 settee, with cushions (R.)
1 side table (L.)
1 armchair, with cushions (L).
1 cabinet at back (R.C.).
1 small round occasional tea table (L. OF SETTEE).
1 wooden chair, with arms (L. OF TABLE).
1 low bookstand, or occasional table, with telephone (DOWN L.).
OTHER FURNITURE TO DRESS, AS DESIRED.

PROPERTIES:
    ON THE ROUND TABLE: a bowl of flowers.
    ON SETTEE AND ARMCHAIR: some ladies' magazines.

Mrs Moggs: cap, coarse apron, bucket and mop.
Ready off l. (for Pauline): tea tray, with afternoon tea for three or four persons.

LIGHTING

All circuits full in floats and battens.
Flood exterior mingled white and No. 3 straw.
Amber lengths on interior backing.
No Cues.

THE TINDER GIRL
(A Miniature Ghost Story)

CHARACTERS

MRS RAWSTEN
HETTIE
MRS ELLERBY
JANET ELLERBY
THE TINDER GIRL

SCENE.—A room in an old inn on the Yorkshire moors.
TIME.—An evening in December.

THE TINDER GIRL

SCENE. — A room leading to a bedroom in an old Yorkshire inn. A December evening.

The room is almost bare of furniture. The walls, though clean, are not newly distempered. There is a door up L. to the landing and another up R. to the bedroom. Down R.C. is an old round table in dark oak or mahogany. An old chair with arms stands above it and another similar to L. of it. At R. is a chest, or tallboy, on which is a shaded lamp. Below it, curtains indicate a window, where there is also a window seat. Only the R. half of the room is lighted, the rest is in comparative shadow. At L., in a small grate, the fire is laid, but not lighted. Below it, the wall is recessed and there is space for the exit of a character.

(See the Ground Plan at the end of the Play.)

When the CURTAIN rises, MRS RAWSTEN, a buxom, grey-haired woman, is at the table, putting two pillows into pillow-cases. HETTIE, a pale-faced young servant girl, enters L., and crosses to C., carrying two blankets.

HETTIE (*checking at* C.). Here are the blankets, Mrs Rawsten.

MRS RAWSTEN. About time — what *have* you been doing?

HATTIE. I had to go up in the attic to get them.

MRS RAWSTEN (*with heavy sarcasm*). Oh — I thought perhaps you'd gone for a couple of sheep to make 'em from. Oh, go on! Don't stand there — take 'em in and put 'em on the bed, and come back for these.

HATTIE. They haven't been aired.

MRS RAWSTEN. Can't help that. I've put a couple of hot-water bottles in, so perhaps they won't notice. Where are they by the way?

HATTIE. The hot-water bottles?

MRS RAWSTEN. No, stupid — the two ladies.

HETTIE. Oh! (*Moving* R.) Just finishing their supper.

(*She exits* R., *to the bedroom.*)

MRS RAWSTEN (*raising her voice for* HETTI'S *benefit*). I expect they'll want to go to bed right away — looked fair worn out, they did. (*She is busy fastening the tapes of the pillow-cases.*)

(HETTIE *enters.*)

HETTIE (*moving to* C.). The young one told me they'd lost their way across the moor — been walking for miles, they said. Said that when they saw the lights of this place, they were never more relieved in their lives.

MRS RAWSTEN. In that case, perhaps they won't be too particular about the room — or anything else.

HETTIE. You mean about the____?

MRS RAWSTEN (*interrupting*). You know perfectly well what I mean, Hettie. Now, you finish off the bed and I'll go down and tell them the room's ready.

HETTIE (*alarmed*). No — I'll go. Please let me go.

MRS RAWSTEN. What's the matter with you?

HETTIE. I — I don't want to stay up here alone — not at night.

MRS RAWSTEN. Don't be ridiculous, girl. You don't believe all those silly stories about ghosts at your age, do you?

HETTIE. Old Sam Berry said he saw her quite distinctly one night.

MRS RAWSTEN (*interrupting*). Old Sam Berry had probably been drinking too much — as usual.

HETTIE. But lots of people *have* seen her. (*She looks round the room nervously.*)

MRS RAWSTEN (*looking at her, and tossing her head*). Have *you* ever seen her?

HETTIE (*turning, and dropping her eyes, abashed*). N-no.

MRS RAWSTEN. Then wait till you have before you start talking rubbish. (*With amused contempt.*) All right — go on down stairs and tell the ladies the room is ready.

HETTIE. Yes, Mrs Rawsten. (*She turns to go.*)

MRS RAWSTEN. And mind I don't catch you telling *them* these daft tales. I'm not going to have you frightening a couple of customers away.

(*She bustles off* R., *with the two pillows.*)

HETTIE. No, Mrs Rawsten.

(*The wind rises. The curtains flap.* HETTIE *glances around, frightened, yet fascinated.*)

MRS RAWSTEN (*calling from the bedroom*). Have you gone down, Hettie?

HETTIE. I'm just off.

MRS RAWSTEN. Well, don't *dawdle*.

(HETTIE *exits* L. *The wind moans. After a moment voices are heard off* L. *Then* MRS ELLERBY *enters, followed by her daughter* JANET. *They stand just inside, looking around, doubtfully. They are well-dressed in country clothes and carry hats and coats.* MRS ELLERBY *is an erect no-nonsense type of woman of middle-age. Her daughter is an attractive young woman of about twenty.* JANET *closes the door. Then* MRS RAWSTEN *enters* R.)

MRS RAWSTEN (*moving to* C.). Oh, there you are. Everything's ready. Did you enjoy your supper?

MRS ELLERBY. Yes, thank you. (*Crossing to the chair above the table.*) We feel much better.

JANET (*moving down* L.). I was beginning to think we were going to spend the rest of our lives wandering round that awful moor.

MRS RAWSTEN. Ah, it's a bad place for getting lost on — specially when the mist comes down.

MRS ELLERBY (*turning, by the chair*). Do you have many people staying here?

MRS RAWSTEN. No, hardly ever. It's a bit off the beaten track, this place. It's a pub really, you know — not an hotel. We've got this one room — and that's not exactly like the Savoy, is it? Still, what can you expect after three hundred years?

JANET. Three hundred years? It doesn't look as old as that.

MRS RAWSTEN (*to* JANET). It's been altered a lot, of course. But that's when it was first built. Used to be a highwayman's hangout in the old days, so they say.

JANET. How romantic!

MRS RAWSTEN. I don't know about that. Proper lot of cut-throats from all accounts. Just as well you didn't get lost and come here in *those* days. (*She laughs comfortably.*)

MRS ELLERBY (*shivering*). I'm absolutely chilled to the bone. Is there any chance of having a fire?

MRS RAWSTEN (*hesitantly*). A — fire?

MRS ELLERBY. I'm afraid it's a lot of trouble for you.

MRS RAWSTEN (*quickly; pulling herself together*). No — no, not at all. As a matter of fact, it's all laid. I'll send the girl up to put a match to it.

MRS ELLERBY. Thank you. I'm sorry to be so much trouble.

MRS RAWSTEN (*moving* L.). That's all right — no trouble at all. (*At the door.*) I'll send her right up.

(*She exits* L.)

MRS ELLERBY (*looking round disparagingly*). What an awful place! (*She sits above the table.*)

JANET (*moving to* C.). Now don't start grumbling, Mother. We're very lucky to find it.

MRS ELLERBY. No wonder they don't have people staying here very often. (*She stamps her feet.*) My feet are *numbed*.

JANET (*cheerfully; rubbing her hands*). Well, we're going to have a nice warm up before we go to bed. (*She glances round the room and then turns to her mother.*) Did you see those locals staring at us in the bar?

MRS ELLERBY. No manners.

JANET (*turning*). It wasn't that. Actually, they were very polite. It was when that girl — what's her name? Hettie — came in and said the bedroom was ready that they started staring.

MRS ELLERBY (*dryly*). Perhaps they've seen it.

JANET (*sitting on the window seat*). That old man in the corner — "Old Sam" they called him — "Old Sam Berry" — his eyes nearly popped out of his head. "You're not sleeping *there*, miss, are you," he said, "not in *that* room?"

MRS ELLERBY. He probably knew the bed would be damp — and I've a feeling he was right.

JANET. Perhaps it's haunted. (*She jumps up.*) I say, what fun!

MRS ELLERBY. Nonsense.

JANET (*arguing*). Three hundred years old? (*Easing to* R. *of the table.*) The meeting-place of cut-throats and highwaymen? Absolutely ideal. (*Moving to* C.) I bet it's absolutely stiff with headless horsemen and clanking chains. It's old enough, anyway. (*She turns to* MRS ELLERBY.)

MRS ELLERBY. And you're old enough to know better.

JANET. What about that time we stayed with the Mountforts in that old castle of theirs? Nothing but moans and groans all night.

MRS ELLERBY. Your father was suffering from indigestion.

JANET (*sitting* L. *of the table*). Mother, you've no sense of the romantic. It's *I* who should be all modern and sneering at the idea of ghosts — *you* should be cringing in a corner at the very thought. (*She takes out her cigarette-case.*)

MRS ELLERBY. When I see a ghost with my own eyes, I'll cringe — not before.

(*There is a knock at the door.*)

Come in.

(JANET *puts down her case, and turns in her chair. The* TINDER GIRL *enters. She is tall, dark and pallidly beautiful. She wears an old-fashioned black dress with a full skirt sweeping the ground. When she moves, she glides rather than walks and never at any time does she look the others full in the face.*)

Oh, you've come to light the fire. Good — I'm absolutely frozen.

(*Without a word, the* TINDER GIRL *glides to the fireplace and kneels before it. From a pocket in her skirt she takes an old-fashioned flint-and-tinder box and strikes sparks from it. Almost immediately the fire glows into life. She watches it in silence for a moment, then rises as if ready to go.)*

JANET (*rising*). I say, excuse me . . .

(*The* TINDER GIRL *pauses, but does not turn, standing motionless in the fireglow.* JANET *eases to* C.)

Do you know this place well?

TINDER GIRL (*still watching the fire*). Yes — very well.

JANET. Have you lived here long?

TINDER GIRL. Yes.

JANET. Then perhaps you can settle a little argument I'm having with my mother. Is this place haunted?

(*The* TINDER GIRL *turns.*)

TINDER GIRL. Yes — it is haunted.

JANET (*turning delightedly; to* MRS ELLERBY). There you are, Mother — what did I tell you?

MRS ELLERBY. Rubbish.

JANET (*turning to the* TINDER GIRL). Do tell us about the ghost. Is it a man or a woman? (*She sits on the lower arm of her chair.*)

TINDER GIRL. A woman.

JANET. Young or old?

TINDER GIRL. Young.

JANET. Beautiful?

TINDER GIRL (*with a faint smile*). So some said.

JANET. What is the story? Do you know it?

TINDER GIRL. Yes — I know it. It is the story of a woman who loved — unwisely.

JANET (*thrilled*). How absolutely wonderful? Do go on.

MRS ELLERBY (*reprovingly*). Janet! She may have something else to do.

TINDER GIRL. No — there is nothing.

JANET. Then do please tell us the story. Who was she — this ghost?

TINDER GIRL. She was married to the earl who ruled over this part of the country. But he was old and ugly and cruel — and she hated him.

JANET. So she fell in love with someone else?

TINDER GIRL. The earl had a younger brother. He was everything that the earl was not — handsome, kind, gentle. They fell in love — yes.

JANET (*prompting*). And then?

TINDER GIRL. And then — the earl discovered what was happening and put them into dungeons, dark caves dug deep into the rock, and left them there to die. But instead of dying, they escaped and fled across the moor — to this place, where they hoped to find help, or at least sympathy. Instead, they found treachery. The men here — cruel, wicked men — held them whilst they sent word to the earl.

JANET. What did he do?

TINDER GIRL. He killed his brother. (*Sombrely.*) The girl he gave to the highwaymen.

JANET. Oh, how terrible.

(*A slight pause.*)

TINDER GIRL. They locked her in this room while they diced for who should take her first.

JANET. In this room?

(*The* TINDER GIRL *slowly looks round the room.*)

TINDER GIRL. It was different then. You see, she killed herself with the only weapon she had — a tinder-box — by setting the place afire.

MRS ELLERBY (*distastefully*). What a dreadful story.

TINDER GIRL. Yes.

JANET (*rising, and easing to* C.). And she — the tinder-box girl — has haunted the place ever since, is that it?

TINDER GIRL. Yes. Ever since, she has — haunted this place. (*Her eyes go to the fireplace.*)

JANET. And has anybody ever seen her?

(*A pause. Then the* TINDER GIRL *looks at* JANET.)

TINDER GIRL. Yes — those who, like herself, are to die by fire.

JANET (*struck by her tone*). Oh. (*She looks at the* GIRL *with interest.*)

MRS ELLERBY (*rising*). I've never heard such an improbable story in all my life. (*She moves down* R., *and peers through the curtains.*)

(JANET *turns to her mother.*)

JANET. Really, Mother — you are the most unbelieving person I've ever met——

(*During the next two speeches the* TINDER GIRL *glides down* L., *and off, into the shadows. Neither* MRS ELLERBY *nor* JANET *see her go.*)

MRS ELLERBY (*still peering out*). Where ghost stories are concerned — yes.

JANET. But you've just heard her say that lots of people have seen this girl. (*She turns to address the* TINDER GIRL.) You *did* say they had, didn't . . . (*she breaks off, in astonishment.*) Why, she's gone!

MRS ELLERBY (*turning from the window*). Back to the kitchen, I imagine, to think of some more stories for credulous young women.

JANET. Poor girl — I expect you upset her.

MRS ELLERBY (*easing below and* R. *of the table; generously*). Well, we can leave her a nice tip in the morning and tell her how much we enjoyed her story.

JANET (*moving above the table*). That's the least we can do. (*Carrying the chair above the table to above the hearth.*) Let's get to the fire.

(MRS RAWSTEN *enters.*)

MRS RAWSTEN (*moving to* C.; *apologetically*). Sorry to have been so long — I couldn't find the matches.

MRS ELLERBY. That's all right, Mrs Rawsten — your girl has been up to light the fire.

MRS RAWSTEN (*surprised*). What? (*She stares at the fire-place, where the fire still flickers and glows.*) But she couldn't have. . . . (*She breaks off, greatly puzzled.*)

MRS ELLERBY. What do you mean?

MRS RAWSTEN. She's been down in the cellars — I know, because I saw her there. And she couldn't have come up without passing me.

MRS ELLERBY (*laughing*). Well, she evidently *did!*

MRS RAWSTEN (*her bewilderment increasing*). I can't understand it because . . . (*She goes to the door and calls.*) Hettie. *Hettie.*

HETTIE (*off; very distant*). What is it?

MRS RAWSTEN (*calling*). Come up here a minute. (*She returns to* C. *to* MRS ELLERBY.) Well! She's down there *now.* If she's been up and lit the fire and gone down again, she's been moving faster than I've ever known her do.

JANET (*moving* R. *of the chair above the hearth*). She stayed up here — quite a time. Didn't she, Mother?

MRS ELLERBY. Yes — five minutes or so.

MRS RAWSTEN (*easing to* L. *of the table, above the chair*).

Well — it's got me beat. I don't see how she could have done.

(HETTIE *enters up* L., *and comes to* C.)

Ah, here she is.

JANET (*cutting in*). Oh, it wasn't that one.

MRS RAWSTEN. *What?*

JANET. It was a different girl.

(HETTIE *looks at* JANET, *then at* MRS RAWSTEN.)

MRS RAWSTEN. It couldn't have been — she's the only girl here. (*She turns to* HETTIE.) Where have you been for the past ten minutes?

HETTIE (*surprised*). Down in the cellars, Mrs Rawsten — you saw me there.

MRS RAWSTEN. D'you mean you haven't been up here to light this fire?

HETTIE. Me? No — how could I?

JANET. The girl who came up here wasn't a bit like her — she was tall and dark and wore a kind of long sweeping skirt.

MRS RAWSTEN (*startled*). What!

(HETTIE *gasps and retreats a pace up stage.*)

JANET. Rather a strange type, as a matter of fact — she lit the fire with a tinder-box.

MRS RAWSTEN (*retreating a pace*). No! It couldn't be! It couldn't!

(HETTIE *whimpers a little.*)

MRS ELLERBY. What's the matter?

MRS RAWSTEN. That — that was *her*. (*With a pace*

forward, twisting her hands.) The Tinder Girl! You've seen her!

MRS ELLERBY. You're not trying to tell me ... Oh, nonsense!

MRS RAWSTEN. But there isn't anyone else in the place, I tell you — only Hettie and me.

JANET (*softly*). The Tinder Girl! Of course!

MRS ELLERBY. If you think I'm going to believe I've seen a ghost you're very much mistaken. Besides — who ever heard of a ghost lighting a fire?

HETTIE (*with almost a scream*). Look!

(*She points to the fire. As she does so it dies down and goes out. For a moment they all stand staring in astonishment. Then* JANET *goes quickly to the fireplace and puts her hand in the grate.*)

JANET (*in an awed voice*). It's cold — stone cold. And look ...

(*As* HETTIE *and* MRS RAWSTEN *edge towards her a pace or two, she takes a handful of paper and sticks out of the grate.*)

It's not burnt — not even scorched. *There hasn't been a fire here.* (*She drops the paper and sticks, and rises.*)

MRS ELLERBY (*easing to* C.). Nonsense — I saw it with my own eyes.

JANET. Did you, Mother? *What* did you see?

(MRS ELLERBY *goes to the fireplace and examines the unburnt paper and sticks for herself, rises and turns.*)

MRS ELLERBY (*perplexed*). I can't understand it. (*Crossing to* R.C.) I swear there was a fire here a few minutes ago, but ... (*She breaks off, sits slowly in the chair* L. *of the table, staring out before her.*)

(JANET *crosses slowly, in silence, and stands above and* L. *of* MRS ELLERBY'S *chair.*)

JANET (*slowly*). Not a few *minutes* ago, Mother — three hundred years ago.

MRS ELLERBY (*rousing herself*). Really, Janet, I can't ...

JANET (*interrupting*). And do you remember what she said? Only those see her who, like herself, are to — die by fire.

MRS ELLERBY *turns slowly in her chair to* JANET. *They look at each other in scared silence.* HETTIE *utters a frightened sob.* MRS RAWSTEN *stares out front, as*—

the CURTAIN *falls.*

FURNITURE AND PROPERTY PLOT

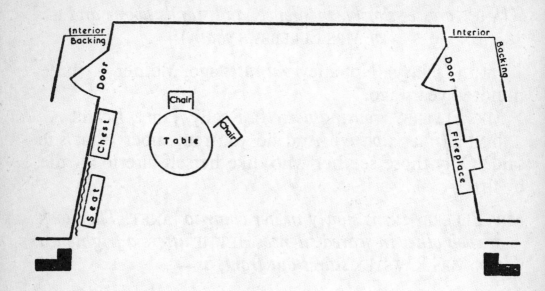

Stage cloth, or shabby carpet. Old rug at fireplace. Window curtain.
ON THE WALLS: one, or two, old-fashioned cheap pictures.
1 small table (preferably round) (DOWN R.C.)
2 old wooden chairs, with arms (ABOVE AND L. OF TABLE).
Chest, or tallboy (or oblong table) (R.). ON IT: shaded oil lamp.
Window seat, or oblong stool (DOWN R.).
Small iron fender at fireplace. Fire laid ready for lighting

PROPERTIES:
    ON THE TABLE: 2 pillows, 2 pillow slips.
    READY OFF L.: 2 folded bed blankets for HETTIE.
    MRS ELLERBY AND JANET: autumn hats and coats, small handbags.
    JANET: cigarette-case.
    TINDER GIRL: tinder-box.

LIGHTING

FLOATS (R. TO C.): No. 51 gold and No. 18 blue, at ½. (C. TO L.): No. 18 blue only, at ¼.

BATTENS (R. TO C.): No. 51 gold and No. 18 blue, at ½. (C. TO L.): No. 18 blue only, at ½.

No. 1 BATTEN SPOT: No. 51 Gold on and around table (R.C.).

No. 17 steel to fade in on TINDER GIRL and fade out on her exit.

INTERIOR BACKING: amber lengths.

FIRE SPOT: to open, OUT. ON CUE: fade in yellow or straw. Add orange and/or red as fire glows up. Quick fade out on 2ND CUE.

THE SITTER-IN
(A Miniature Crime Comedy)

CHARACTERS

MRS MARY JOHNSON
LILY SMITH
MISS TRIPLOW
DR ETHEL CARDEN
MRS BOWSER

SCENE. — The JOHNSONS' Flat.
TIME. — The present.

THE SITTER-IN

SCENE. — The living-room of the JOHNSONS' flat. Evening.

It is an elegant room, much decorated with silverware, cut-glass ornaments and objets d'art. At the back, L.C., is an arch, the curtains of which are open, leading to the hall. The front door is presumed to be to L., a few feet from the arch. A hallstand can be seen. There is another door, down R., leading to a bedroom. The window is at L., down stage. At R.C. is a settee. At L.C., above the level of the window, is a gate-legged table, with a runner and a fine silver bowl. There are chairs above, R., and L. of the table. Above the settee is a small table with a telephone. At the back, R.C., a side table with drinks and glasses, etc. Other furniture to dress as desired.

(See the Ground Plan at the end of the Play.)

When the CURTAIN rises, the lights are on. MRS MARY JOHNSON, young, and smartly dressed in an evening gown and fur cape, carrying a dainty evening bag, is standing below the settee, giving last-minute instructions to LILY SMITH, a prim female seated R. of the table. LILY has a sallow complexion, scragged back hair, and a quiet, respectful demeanour which matches her plain black dress.

MARY. Now, you're sure you know where everything is?

LILY. Yes, ma'm.

MARY. If the baby cries, give him some rose-hips and sit him up for five minutes.

LILY. Yes, ma'm.

MARY (*a shade anxiously*). You have done baby-sitting before, haven't you?

LILY. Oh yes, ma'm — frequently.

(MARY *sits on the settee, and looks for her compact in her handbag.*)

MARY. It's funny we've never come across you — I thought we knew all the sitters-in around here. (*She finds her compact.*)

LILY. I heard there was a shortage of them in this district, ma'm — that's why I wrote to you.

MARY (*attending to her face*). I'm very glad you did. What with the maid being away and my regular girl booked up, I don't know *what* I would have done. (*Putting her compact away and her bag on the settee.*) By the way, how did you get hold of my name and address?

LILY. A lady gave them to me. I forget her name for the moment, but she said she was a friend of yours — used to be at school with you, I think she said.

MARY. Well, I'm very much obliged to her — whoever she was. (*She glances at her wrist-watch.*) Good gracious — it's nearly eight o'clock — I must fly!

LILY (*rising*). What time will you be back, ma'm?

MARY. Oh, about midnight. (*She goes to the door down* L., *peeps through and then moves again to* R.C.) I don't really like leaving him — but I suppose he'll be all right with you — I mean, you being a stranger.

LILY. I'm sure he will, ma'am.

MARY. Well, I'd better hurry. See you later. Good-bye. (*She goes out into the hall.*)

LILY. Good-bye, ma'm.

(MARY *checks in the doorway, evidently seeing something by the front door which surprises her. She turns to* LILY.)

MARY (*laughing*). You *have* got some luggage! Two bags for one night!

LILY. I'm going on to my sister at Bournemouth in the morning.

MARY. Oh — I see! Good-bye.

(*She disappears. The front door is heard to slam. Immediately* LILY *drops her demure manner. She crosses up to the drinks table, pours herself a drink, swallows it at a gulp, and looks round the room speculatively as she lights a cigarette. Then she eases down to the settee table and dials a number on the telephone.*)

LILY (*into the telephone; in brisk hard tones very unlike her voice hitherto.*) That you, Alf? ... She's just gone — won't be back till midnight. ... Yes, plenty of time. ... Well now, listen — I've had a good look round and there's masses of good stuff here, masses. I'll pick out the best, shove it into a couple of suitcases and have them ready by the time you get here. Bring the car round right away and I'll pass the cases out of the window. ... That's right. ... And when you get here, whistle like you were looking for a dog, so's I'll know it's you ... And get a move on — this is the best joint we've done yet.

(*She rings off. Then, after helping herself to another quick drink, she goes into the hall, returning a moment later with two suitcases, into which she begins to pack the more valuable ornaments. The front door buzzer sounds.* LILY *looks up in alarm, thrusts the bags hastily under the table, and goes out into the hall, to* L.)

MISS TRIPLOW (*off*). Oh, *thank* you! I just want a word with Mrs Johnson.

LILY (*off*). But she's not . . .

(MISS TRIPLOW *enters and moves down* R.C. *She is an elderly, gushing spinster, with a girlish giggle and a habit of talking in italics.* LILY *follows her on.*)

MISS TRIPLOW (*entering*). It's quaite all raight!

LILY (*sharply*). Mrs Johnson's out.

MISS TRIPLOW. Oh dear — how *tiresome*. (*She turns down* R.C.) Do you know, that's *just* like me! If ever I call on someone, that someone is *sure* to be out. I have an absolute *genius* for picking the wrong moment. (*She looks at* LILY, *as if seeing her for the first time.*) Let me see, do I know you?

LILY (*coming* L.C.; *suppressing her impatience with an effort*). I don't think so, ma'm — I'm the new sitter-in.

MISS TRIPLOW (*gushing*). Really? Oh, how *wonderful!* I mean, to spend one's time looking after the little ones — so *elevating*, if you know what I mean.

LILY. Yes, ma'm. Are you a friend of Mrs Johnson's?

MISS TRIPLOW (*girlishly*). Oh dear — of *course* you've no *idea* who I am, have you? I mean, you don't know me from *Adam*, do you? Or perhaps I should say, from Eve. (*She giggles.*) I mean, I might be *anybody*, mightn't I? A burglar or something. . . . You never can tell, can you?

LILY (*grimly*). No, you can't.

MISS TRIPLOW. But you can set your mind *completely* at rest. I'm Miss Triplow, and I live in the flat upstairs, and I've just popped down to borrow a little butter.

LILY. Butter?

MISS TRIPLOW. Just a teeny-weeny piece — for my Tabbykins' supper, you know — he simply won't *touch* margarine — *quite* the little epicure, he is. Mind you, I . . .

LILY (*interrupting impatiently*). I'll see if I can find you some.

MISS TRIPLOW. Oh, *would* you? That *is* kind.

LILY (*curtly*). Not at all.

(*She exits to the hall off* R. MISS TRIPLOW *prowls inquisitively about the room. She comes across the glass on the table from which* LILY *had her drinks and sniffs at it suspiciously.* LILY *re-enters, carrying a small packet.*)

MISS TRIPLOW (*turning, down* L.C.). Oh, you've found some. How clever of you!

LILY (*moving down* C.). Will this be enough?

MISS TRIPLOW. Oh, yes — *ample*.

LILY. Glad to have been of service, ma'm. Good night.

MISS TRIPLOW (*reluctant to go*). Oh — well — good night. (*Easing to* C.) If you feel lonely, just knock on the ceiling.

LILY. I shan't feel lonely.

MISS TRIPLOW. I know! I'll bring Tabbykins down and then we can play a game of bezique!

LILY (*tersely*). I'm afraid I don't know it.

MISS TRIPLOW. Oh, it's *awfully* easy! Four kings, eighty; simple marriage, twenty. . . . I'll be back in a minute. (*She moves up towards the hall.*)

LILY. I don't think you'd better.

MISS TRIPLOW (*pausing*). Oh? (*Turning.*) Why not?

LILY (*thinking fast*). Well — er — as a matter of fact . . (*With sudden inspiration.*) The baby's not very well.

MISS TRIPLOW. Oh, *poor* little cherub! What's the matter — a pain in his little tum-tum?

LILY. No, it's — er — scarlet fever.

MISS TRIPLOW (*alarmed*). Scarlet fever?

LILY. Yes, I'm afraid so.

MISS TRIPLOW. Oh dear — how dreadful!

LILY. It's very infectious, you know. And I would suggest, unless you want to run the risk of Tabbykins getting it, the less you expose yourself to infection . . .

MISS TRIPLOW (*nervously*). Yes, yes. Quite so, quite so. (*She breaks off, distressed.*) Oh dear! Well — thank you for warning me.

LILY. Not at all. (*She edges* MISS TRIPLOW *towards the door.*)

MISS TRIPLOW (*pausing in the doorway*). Do you think I ought to gargle?

LILY. Yes — immediately. For an hour.

MISS TRIPLOW. Oh dear. . . .

(*She hurries out, feeling her throat.* LILY *follows, with a contemptuous smile, closes the front door, and returns. She drags out the bags and resumes packing them. After a moment or two the door buzzer sounds again. With a smothered exclamation,* LILY *bundles the cases under the table again, smoothes her dress, goes out, and returns with* DR ETHEL CARDEN, *a mannish, middle-aged woman dressed in outdoor clothes and carrying a doctor's bag. We hear her say, "Evening. I'm Dr Carden." Then the front door slams. She moves into the room followed by* LILY.)

DR CARDEN (*putting her case on the settee and turning*). Just met that Triplow woman on the stairs. Tells me the baby's got scarlet fever.

LILY (*disconcerted*). Oh! I — er . . .

DR CARDEN. Complete nonsense, of course. Saw the child only this morning. Nothing the matter with it then. Still, better have a look, I suppose.

(*She exits to the room down* R. LILY *fumbles under the*

80

table, taking the loot out of the suitcases and putting the ornaments back in their places. DR CARDEN *re-enters.*)

Scarlet fever my foot! Child's as right as ninepence. Who are you, anyway?

LILY (*down* L.C.). I'm the new sitter-in, Doctor.

DR CARDEN. Oh. Not been here before?

LILY. No, Doctor.

DR CARDEN. Well, if that fool of a Triplow woman comes down here again, tell her not to waste my time.

LILY. Yes, Doctor.

DR CARDEN. Old maid's delusions — that's what's the matter with her. Always imagining burglars under the bed — and being damn disappointed when she doesn't find any. You look fidgety — what's the matter with you?

LILY. Nothing, Doctor.

DR CARDEN. Want a tonic, I expect. Everybody wants a tonic. Me in particular. Yes — that's an idea. (*She moves to the hall.*) Good night.

LILY (*following*). Good night, Doctor.

(*They exit. The front door is heard to close.* LILY *re-enters and once again tackles the suitcases — with a kind of irritable haste. The door buzzer sounds again.* LILY *stops her packing and glares at the hall entrance.*)

(*Moving up; calling crossly.*) Who is it?

MISS TRIPLOW (*off*). Me.

LILY (*irritably*). What do you want?

MISS TRIPLOW (*off*). I want to ask you something. It's important.

(LILY *hesitates angrily for a moment, then, moving down, throws a cloth over the suitcases, runs into the hall and opens the door off* L.)

LILY (*off*). Well?

MISS TRIPLOW (*off*). I wanted to ask if you thought it was all right to give Tabbykins that butter — or do you think it's infected?

LILY. Of course it's infected. And I advise you to give it to him. (*She slams the door, off* L., *reappears in the entrance, turns, and calls after* MISS TRIPLOW.) And take some yourself!

(*Her nerves frayed by the interruptions, she braces herself and tackles the suitcases once more; one of these is now full. Then the buzzer sounds again.* LILY *throws a cloth furiously over the cases, dashes into the hall, and returns with* MRS BOWSER. *The latter is a slatternly charwoman armed with a bucket, brooms, and a mop. She checks at* C., *and turns.* LILY *is regarding her with exasperated astonishment.*)

What do you want?

MRS BOWSER. I've come to clean it up. (*She looks around the room.*) Well, where is it?

LILY. Where's *what*?

MRS BOWSER. That's a daft question, I must say. What I've come here to do, of course.

LILY. I haven't the faintest idea who you are or what you're talking about.

MRS BOWSER. I'm Mrs Bowser and I've come to clean up the mess.

LILY (*exasperated*). *What* mess?

MRS BOWSER. The mess that's 'ere. The one you want cleaning up.

LILY (*with suppressed fury*). Now look here, Mrs Mouser, or Towser, or whatever your name is — I don't know anything about any mess and if I did I wouldn't want *you* to clean it up.

MRS BOWSER (*aggrieved*). That's a nice thing, I must say. Just going 'ome I was, when someone phoned down and said there was a mess in Number Forty-six that 'ad to be cleaned up right away.

LILY. Well, there isn't. You must have got the number wrong.

MRS BOWSER. That's right — blame me! Just doing my job, I was . . .

LILY. Will you please *go*.

MRS BOWSER (*reluctantly gathering up her equipment*). Fetched all the way from the basement. . . .

LILY (*raging*). *Will — you — get — out.*

MRS BOWSER (*going, but still grumbling*). Don't know what things are coming to, I don't — come up all this way — lot of mucking about — fine thing . . .

(*Still muttering to herself she exits. LILY leans against the doorway, exhausted. A baby begins to cry, off R.*)

LILY. That's right — now *you* start!

(*She exits to the room down R. In her haste she has left the front door ajar. MISS TRIPLOW enters cautiously, looks round, tiptoes to the table, and peeps under the cloth covering the suitcases. The baby stops crying. MISS TRIPLOW rummages in the suitcases. LILY re-enters and stands transfixed as she sees what MISS TRIPLOW is doing.*)

What are you up to?

(*MISS TRIPLOW jumps, and turns to LILY.*)

MISS TRIPLOW. I — er — I — er . . . (*She gathers her*

courage in both hands.) I think the question should be, What are *you* doing?

LILY (*moving to* R.C.; *curtly*). None of your business.

MISS TRIPLOW (*boldly*). Oh, but it *is*. You're muscling in on *my* racket.

LILY (*astounded*). What?

MISS TRIPLOW. You heard. Sit down — I want to talk to you. (*She moved up* C.)

(LILY, *bewildered, sits on the settee.*)

(*Severely.*) Giving me all that stuff about scarlet fever! Why didn't you tell me you were on the pinch?

LILY. And what would you have said if I had?

MISS TRIPLOW. I'd have said to myself, "Triplow, my girl — you've been left at the post. Someone has got in before you."

LILY (*incredulously*). Do you mean to say *you* were casing this joint?

MISS TRIPLOW. What do you think?

LILY (*staggered*). Well, I'm . . .

MISS TRIPLOW. (*cutting in*). I expect you are. But never mind about that. (*She nods towards the suitcases.*) Hadn't you better get on with your packing?

LILY (*rising; still dazed*). Yes — I — I suppose I had.

(*She crosses* L. *and begins on the second suitcase again. Unobserved by her,* MISS TRIPLOW *moves into the hall surreptitiously, bolts the front door and returns.*)

MISS TRIPLOW (*as* LILY *is about to put a silver ornament in the case*). Don't bother with that one. It's only electroplate.

LILY (*staring at it*). How do you know?

MISS TRIPLOW. As you said just now. I've already — er — cased the joint. Here's a better one — "Present from

Margate". (*She picks up a china ornament from the side table up* L.C.)

LILY (*suspiciously*). What are you talking about? That isn't worth fourpence. (*She closes one suitcase.*)

MISS TRIPLOW. Oh, yes it is. Listen. (*She shakes the ornament. It rattles.*) Real sovereigns. Saving them up for the baby. I know — because I suggested it.

LILY (*admiringly*). Say, you're real smart, aren't you?

MISS TRIPLOW. You've got to be in this racket.

(*Suddenly, off stage, there comes a sound of someone whistling to a dog.* LILY *looks up sharply.*)

Who's that? Your boy friend, I suppose. Come on — shove that stuff out of the window. (*She puts the ornament on the table.*)

(LILY *opens the window and peers out.*)

LILY. I can't see him. (*She picks up one suitcase and returns to the window.*)

MISS TRIPLOW (*moving down* L.C.). Never mind — just drop it out. (*She picks up the other suitcase.*) Here's the other one.

(LILY *drops the first suitcase out of the window.* MISS TRIPLOW *hands her the other one. The door buzzer goes.*)

MARY (*off*). Miss Triplow — Miss Triplow — are you there?

LILY (*alarmed*). Who's that?

MISS TRIPLOW. It's Mrs Johnson! Come on, you'd better get out of here quick. Through the window. Make a run for it. It's not far to drop.

(LILY *drops the other suitcase out of the window and scram-*

bles after it. The door buzzer goes again. Someone starts hammering on the door and shouting. From off stage comes the sounds of police whistles and hoarse shouts.)

(*Shouting out of the window.*) There she is. Go on, after her. Go on. Go on. *Got her.* That's the stuff.

(*The hammering on the door increases and* MISS TRIPLOW *reluctantly withdraws from the window, runs into the hall, and unbolts the front door.* MARY *hurries in, followed by* DR CARDEN, MRS BOWSER, *and* MISS TRIPLOW.)

MARY (*running to down* R.C.). What on earth's happening? (*Turning.*) Miss Triplow!

MISS TRIPLOW (*following her down; calmly*). Just a small case of burglary — your sitter-in.

MARY. What!

(DR CARDEN *moves down to* L.C., *below the table*; MRS BOWSER *to above the chair* R. *of the table.*)

MISS TRIPLOW. Did the police pick you up at the station?
MARY. Yes, but . . .
MISS TRIPLOW (*cutting in*). Good! I told them that's where they'd find you.
MARY. But I don't understand.
MISS TRIPLOW. It's quite simple, really. As soon as you'd gone, she telephoned. But she didn't know we'd got a party line, you see. And I heard every word she said.
MARY. Good heavens! What did you do?
MISS TRIPLOW. As soon as she'd finished, I phoned the police. But I had to do something to keep her here until they arrived.
DR CARDEN. So that's why you sent me in about the baby?

MRS BOWSER. And me about the cleaning?

MISS TRIPLOW (*apologetically*). Yes. I'm awfully sorry. But I *had* to do *something*, hadn't I? I even had to pretend *I* was a burglar, too. Can you *imagine*?

DR CARDEN (*sourly*). Burglars on the brain.

MISS TRIPLOW. Now, if you'll excuse me, I'd better go and see the police — I expect they'll want my evidence.

MARY (*anxiously*). Don't you think you ought to rest a while? I mean, after all this excitement?

MISS TRIPLOW (*bracing herself a little*). Rest? Good gracious, whatever for? (*Uncertainly.*) I — I never felt better in my . . .

(*She collapses in a dead faint on the settee. The others gather round anxiously, fanning her and patting her hand.*)

CURTAIN.

FURNITURE AND PROPERTY PLOT

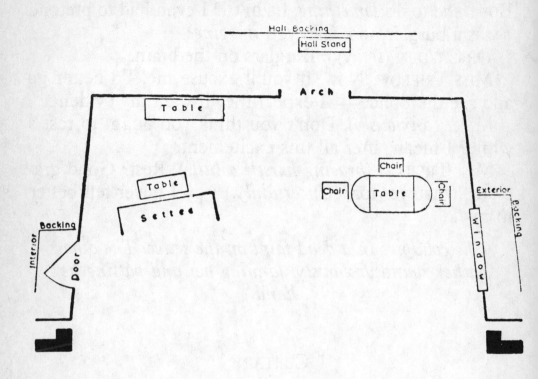

Carpet on the stage. Strip in the hall. Heavy curtains at window, and arch.

On the walls: Some good pictures — etchings and water-colours.

1 settee, with cushions (R.C.).

1 gate-legged table (L.C.). On it: runner, a good silver bowl or other centre-piece.

1 small table above settee. On it: dial telephone.

1 side table (back R.C.). On it: various drinks and glasses.

3 small chairs around table.

Hat-and-coat stand in the hall.

Other furniture as desired, to accommodate props.

PROPERTIES:

On tables and elsewhere, a number of ornaments, silver, and various valuables as directed by producer. Also cigarettes and matches.

IN THE HALL AT OPENING: 2 empty suitcases, an old cloth in each.

MARY: evening handbag with compact, etc.

Ready off up R.: paper packet to contain butter (LILY).

DR CARDEN: doctor's small bag.

MRS BOWSER: bucket, broom, mop.

SOUND EFFECTS:

Front door buzzer (OFF L.).

Man whistling (OFF L.).

Baby crying (OFF R.).

Shouts, police whistles, hammering on door (OFF L.).

LIGHTING

FLOATS: No. 51 gold, No. 7 pink, No. 18 blue at ½. (C. SECTION PINK MAY BE FULL, FOR FIRE GLOW.)

BATTENS: No. 51 gold, No. 7 pink, No. 18 blue, at ¾. (THESE MAY BE CHECKED TO ½ IF ADEQUATE BATTEN SPOTS USED.)

BATTEN SPOTS: No. 51 gold on R.C. and L.C. areas.

IN HALL: amber lengths, checked well down, or gold spot as from hall lamp.

INTERIOR BACKING (R.): faint pink glow only.

EXTERIOR BACKING: No. 17 steel, checked down.

NO CUES.

JEANNIE
(A Miniature Drama)

CHARACTERS

OLIVE
MRS MATTHEWS
MRS BLUNDELL
THE NURSE
JEANNIE

SCENE. — A bed-sitting-room in a cheap lodging house.
TIME. — An autumn afternoon.

JEANNIE

SCENE. — A bed-sitting-room in a cheap lodging house. An autumn afternoon.

Although not poverty-stricken, it is a poor room, meagrely furnished. There is a door at the back, C. At R., a single bed faces down stage. Up L., curtains drawn across suggest the presence of another bed hidden by them. Curtains, down R., indicate a window. Down L. are a cheap dressing table and a chair. There is a small trunk on the floor, down R. and a small table R. of the bed. A small oblong table stands L.C., with two small chairs, R. and above. L. of the bed is a small chair with arms.

(See the Ground Plan at the end of the Play.)

When the CURTAIN rises, MRS MATTHEWS, an elderly woman, frail and wan, is in the bed up R. Her daughter OLIVE, about thirty, is seated L. of the bed reading aloud to her. OLIVE has a strong, intelligent face, but is not pretty in the accepted sense. Her clothes match the poverty of the room; they are worn, but respectable.

OLIVE (*reading from a book*). ". . . In those silent wintry hours when Romola lay resting from her weariness, her mind, travelling back over the past, and gazing across the undefined distance over the future, saw all objects from a new position. Her experience since the moment . . ."

MRS MATTHEWS (*faintly*). Jeannie. . . .

OLIVE. What did you say, Mother?

MRS MATTHEWS. Jeannie — where's my little Jeannie? (*Her head moves restlessly.*) Jeannie . . . (*She turns fever-*

ishly anxious eyes on OLIVE.) Where is she, Olive? Why doesn't she come?

OLIVE (*soothingly*). She will, Mother.

MRS MATTHEWS. But when? It's so long — so long . . .

OLIVE. She's away, dear — travelling.

MRS MATTHEWS. Where?

OLIVE (*evasively*). Oh, you know what Jeannie is, Mother — rushing about all over the place.

MRS MATTHEWS. Did you write to her? Did you tell her I wanted to see her before I — before I . . .

OLIVE (*breaking in*). Of course I did — she'll come as soon as she can. (*Hastening on.*) Now, Mother — let's get you tidied up before the Nurse gets here. (*Rising; lightly.*) You know what a fuss she is over pillows and things. (*She moves gently and deftly about the bed. It is obvious that all this is merely a pretext to try to change her mother's train of thought. She speaks brightly and cheerfully.*) Did you see the flowers I got for you? Look, over there on the table. (*As she crosses below the bed to* R. *of it.*) I got them from that funny little man in the market — do you remember? (*Adjusting the pillow, etc.*) He asked how you were getting on. I told him you'd soon be up and about again and then perhaps we would . . .

MRS MATTHEWS (*her mind running on her own thoughts*). Jeannie can't have forgotten that I'm ill, can she? It's been so long since she wrote. She couldn't have forgotten, could she?

OLIVE. No, no — of course not. (*She tucks in the quilt.*) I expect the letters got lost in the post. (*She tidies the bedside table.*)

MRS MATTHEWS. Yes — that's it — it must be. My little girl couldn't have forgotten — she couldn't . . .

(*She drowses off.* OLIVE *looks at her, sighs, and turns to the table, picking up the medicine glass. There is a gentle knock at the door, and* MRS BLUNDELL *enters. She is a kindly untidy woman of about fifty.*)

MRS BLUNDELL. The Nurse is just coming, Miss Matthews — I thought I'd let you know. (*She moves to the chair* L. *of the bed.*)

OLIVE. Thank you, Mrs Blundell. (*She moves down and starts to cross* L.)

MRS BLUNDELL. How is she?

OLIVE. About the same. (*She goes to the dressing table and puts down the glass.*)

MRS BLUNDELL (*sympathetically*). Poor dear. Who'd've thought when you first came here — how long ago was it — five years? — that she'd spend four of them like that? I wish there was something I could do.

OLIVE. You've been very kind, Mrs Blundell. If it hadn't been for you, I don't know how we'd've managed.

MRS BLUNDELL. Oh, that's all right, dear — even landladies have hearts, you know. Is there any news from that sister of yours?

OLIVE (*turning away; not wanting to discuss it*). No. (*She tidies the dressing table.*)

MRS BLUNDELL (*crossing to* L.C.. *above the table*). I do think she ought to have written or something. Your mother's very fond of her, isn't she? When I come up here during the day sometimes, while you're at work, she's always talking about her — it's Jeannie this, and Jeannie that. . . .

(*She breaks off as the* NURSE *appears at the door. She is in outdoor clothes and carries a little black bag.*)

NURSE. May I come in?

OLIVE (*turning*). Oh, good morning, Nurse — yes, please do.

MRS BLUNDELL. 'Morning.

NURSE (*moving down* C.). And how is she today?

OLIVE. Much the same. Sleeping at the moment.

(*The* NURSE *goes to the bed and bends over* MRS MATTHEWS, *feeling her pulse and forehead.*)

NURSE. Is she taking her medicine?

OLIVE. Yes.

MRS BLUNDELL. Not that it's doing her much good, poor dear.

OLIVE (*moving below the* L. *end of the table*). Nurse — I wanted to ask you something. I spoke to the doctor the other day, but . . . (*She hesitates.*)

NURSE (*moving from the bed, to* C.). Yes, what is it?

OLIVE (*steadily*). She's dying, isn't she?

NURSE. Oh, we mustn't say that, you know. I've seen patients a good deal worse than this up and about in a few weeks.

OLIVE (*breaking in; not deceived by the* NURSE'S *professional caution*). I've got a little money saved up — about a hundred pounds. . . . Isn't there anything we can do? A nursing-home, perhaps?

NURSE (*shaking her head slowly*). No. She'll do as well here as in any nursing-home. And Dr Macready is quite one of the best on this sort of case. I think we're doing all that can be done. Would you get me a glass of water, please — I want to mix this medicine.

OLIVE (*picking up the glass*). Yes, of course.

(*She crosses up* C. *and exits. The* NURSE *opens her bag on the table and produces some bottles.*)

MRS BLUNDELL (*easing above the* L. *end of the table*). It isn't the medicine she wants.

NURSE (*sitting* R. *of the table*). What do you mean?

MRS BLUNDELL. She's fretting over that other girl of hers, Jeannie. It's too bad of her not to write or come or anything. Selfish, that's what she is — I always did think so. Selfish and spoilt. But do you think her mother could ever see anything wrong in her? Not on your life.

NURSE (*selecting a bottle*). Where is she? Couldn't we send for her?

MRS BLUNDELL (*shrugging*). If we knew where she was, we could. Hasn't been here for six months. It's the old story, Nurse — the pretty young one who gets all the affection, and the other — who does everything and still takes second place.

NURSE (*nodding towards the door*). Do you mean — her?

MRS BLUNDELL. Yes, of course. That money she was talking about — saved it up, she has, shilling by shilling almost, so that she can go to Australia.

NURSE (*examining a bottle against the light*). Why Australia? (*She puts the bottle down and selects another.*)

MRS BLUNDELL. She was in love with a man years ago, and he went there. Wanted her to get married and go with him. But she wouldn't go — because of her mother. "Somebody's got to look after her," she said.

NURSE. What about the younger sister — Jeannie — couldn't she have done it?

MRS BLUNDELL (*scornfully*). Her? She was too busy going to dances and having boy friends.

(*The* NURSE *glances at the bed and speaks in an undertone*
to MRS BLUNDELL.)

NURSE. Well, I shouldn't say this, I suppose — but I
don't think it will be long before she can go to Australia.
MRS BLUNDELL. You mean . . .?
NURSE. Yes. There isn't much hope, I'm afraid. But you
mustn't say anything.
MRS BLUNDELL. No, of course not.

(*She moves across to the bed, looks compassionately at the*
sleeping woman and clicks her tongue sympathetically.
OLIVE *enters, carrying a glass of water, which she gives*
to the NURSE.)

NURSE. Thank you. (*She mixes up a draught of medicine.*)
Give this to her about six o'clock.
OLIVE. Very well.
NURSE. Dr Macready will be here about half past. But
if there is anything urgent before then, you know where
you can get hold of him.
OLIVE. Yes.
NURSE. Just keep her quiet and comfortable. Good
morning.
OLIVE. Good morning, Nurse. And thank you.
MRS BLUNDELL (*to* NURSE). I'll see you out.

(*The* NURSE *and* MRS BLUNDELL *exit.* OLIVE *stands looking*
down at her mother.)

MRS MATTHEWS (*in her sleep*). Jeannie — Jeannie . . .
(*Her voice fades.*)
OLIVE (*sitting by the bed; soothingly*). It's all right, Mother
— I'm here.

(*She takes her mother's wandering hand and strokes it.*

98

MRS MATTHEWS *gradually quietens.* OLIVE *gently releases herself, gets up, and moves softly about the room, tidying. The door opens suddenly, and* JEANNIE *enters. She shuts the door quickly behind her and leans against it, panting. She is young and pretty in a doll-like way. Her clothes are too flashy.*)

OLIVE (*turning in amazement*). Jeannie! (*She rises.*)
JEANNIE (*flatly*). Hullo, Olive.
OLIVE. Jeannie — how did you get in? I didn't hear you.
JEANNIE. Mrs Blundell left the door open when she let the Nurse out. I slipped in and hid till she'd gone.
OLIVE. You hid? Why? From whom?

(JEANNIE *gives a hard laugh and moves down* C. *She turns and looks down at her mother.*)

JEANNIE. How is she?
OLIVE. Not good, Jeannie. I don't think she can last much longer.
JEANNIE. Oh.
OLIVE (*easing down, level with* JEANNIE). She's been asking for you — constantly. Why didn't you write? Or come and see her?
JEANNIE (*curtly*). I couldn't.
OLIVE. Why not? However busy you've been, a letter doesn't take long. Why couldn't you have written?
JEANNIE (*moving to the chair* R. *of the table, flinging herself in it*). I just couldn't, that's all. Don't nag, Olive — I'm just about all in.
OLIVE (*crossing to* L.C., *above the table*). Jeannie — what's happened?
JEANNIE (*evasively*). Happened?

OLIVE. You're in some kind of trouble, aren't you?

(JEANNIE *laughs mirthlessly*.)

JEANNIE. Trouble! You don't know the meaning of the word.

OLIVE. Tell me about it, Jeannie.

JEANNIE. What, and have you say, "I told you so"?

OLIVE. Have I ever said that?

JEANNIE. No, Olive — you've been a good sport. I don't know how you've put up with all this. (*She looks round the room distastefully*.) Do you still hear from Jack?

OLIVE. Yes.

JEANNIE. You were a mug not to have married him when you had the chance.

OLIVE. I couldn't have left mother, Jeannie.

JEANNIE. Supposing she hadn't had you? She'd've had to have managed somehow, wouldn't she?

OLIVE. But she did have me. (*She turns the chair above the table*.)

JEANNIE. Oh, well — if you prefer it that way, that's your business.

OLIVE. Jeannie — (*sitting above the table*) you haven't told me about yourself. Where have you been all these months? What have you been doing?

JEANNIE. Oh, I've been making do — you needn't worry about me.

OLIVE. Are you going to stay here now? Mrs Blundell will find you somewhere for you to sleep.

JEANNIE. No — I can't stay, Olive.

OLIVE. Well, for a little while, anyway — can't you?

JEANNIE. No, I must go. I can't stay, Olive — only a few minutes. (*She looks across at* MRS MATTHEWS.)

OLIVE. A few minutes! (*She rises.*) You can't go without talking to mother.

JEANNIE (*looking down at her hands*). I don't want to talk to her — she'll only ask me questions.

OLIVE (*steadily*). Would they be so difficult to answer?

JEANNIE (*turning to* OLIVE). You think I don't care anything for her, don't you? But I do — in my own way. (*She rises, moves down* R.C., *and turns.*) It's not your way, Olive — I couldn't put up with all this — (*crossing* L.) sickness and being hard up and — and just sort of sitting there waiting for her to die. (*Turning.*) I couldn't do it, Olive — I couldn't. (*She sits by the dressing table.*)

OLIVE (*moving to* R. *of the table*). You must stay and talk to her, Jeannie — it'd break her heart if she knew you'd been here ...

JEANNIE (*quickly*). She needn't know, need she?

OLIVE. Why did you come here?

JEANNIE. I — I want some help.

OLIVE. You always did, Jeannie — even when you were a little girl. But you'd never have the kind of help that people offered you.

(JEANNIE *jumps up; angrily.*)

JEANNIE. That's right, preach at me. I knew you would.

OLIVE. I'm not preaching. (*Easing below the chair* R. *of the table.*) And I'll help you if I can. What is it you want me to do?

JEANNIE. I must have some money. (*She sits again, hopelessly.*)

OLIVE. What do you want it for?

JEANNIE (*fretfully*). What does it matter what for?

OLIVE. I think I'm entitled to know, Jeannie. Tell me.

JEANNIE. No.

OLIVE. Why not?

JEANNIE. If I did, you wouldn't give it to me.

(*There is a silence.* OLIVE *looks steadily at* JEANNIE.)

OLIVE. I'm not going to give you any money unless you tell me what it's for.

JEANNIE (*after a pause*). Very well. I want it to replace some I've stolen. Now you know.

OLIVE (*quietly*). Who did you steal it from?

JEANNIE (*turning a little from* OLIVE'S *gaze*). A friend.

OLIVE. A friend?

JEANNIE. Well, it was a man I met, really. He — he left it lying about and — and I took it.

OLIVE. You're not telling me the truth, are you?

JEANNIE (*looking at her*). Yes, of course I am.

(*Again there is a silence.* OLIVE *looks steadily at* JEANNIE, *whose gaze wavers and falls.*)

OLIVE. Tell me, Jeannie.

JEANNIE. It's Mario's fault, really. He said that . . .

OLIVE (*sharply*). Who is Mario?

JEANNIE. He's the man who owns the club where I work.

OLIVE (*sitting slowly in the chair*). I didn't know you worked in a club.

JEANNIE. It's a place in Soho — one of those dumps where they sell bad whisky after hours to anyone who's mug enough to pay their prices. And they have girls there — "dance hostesses" they call them if they want to be polite, and something else if they don't.

OLIVE. And you were one of them?

JEANNIE. Yes.

OLIVE (*evenly*). Go on.

JEANNIE. Well, one night a man came in — a foreigner

of some kind. He'd had enough to drink when he got there and by the time Mario had finished with him he'd had more than enough. Mario said one of the girls had better take him home.

OLIVE. Wasn't there any male staff there who could have taken him home?

JEANNIE (*impatiently*). Oh, for heaven's sake, Olive — don't be so green!

(*A slight pause.*)

OLIVE. Well, what happened?

JEANNIE. So I took him home — some dingy little hotel where they weren't too particular. Got him into bed and then, well ... (*She breaks off, with a little shrug.*)

OLIVE. You helped yourself to his money?

JEANNIE (*looking down*). Yes.

OLIVE. And then?

JEANNIE (*looking up*). He came round to the club the next night and raised the roof. Said that if I didn't return the money he'd tell the police.

OLIVE. How much was it?

JEANNIE (*after a slight hesitation*). Fifty pounds.

OLIVE (*blankly*). Fifty pounds.

JEANNIE (*petulantly*). Well, you don't think I was doing it for pennies, do you? (*She suddenly bursts into tears.*) Oh, Olive — what am I going to do? (*Rising.*) You will help me, won't you? (*Going to her.*) Say you'll help me?

(*She falls on her knees and clasps* OLIVE *round the legs, looking up at her with tear-stained face.* OLIVE, *with a sudden movement, rises, turns away from her, and stands looking down at the sleeping* MRS MATTHEWS.)

OLIVE. All right, Jeannie — I'll help you. (*She turns to* JEANNIE.) But on one condition.

JEANNIE (*rising*). Anything, Olive, anything. I'll do anything you tell me. I promise.

OLIVE. Mother hasn't got very long to live, Jeannie. You must stay here with us until she — goes.

(JEANNIE *looks round the shabby room.*)

JEANNIE. Oh, Olive — I couldn't. I — I'd go mad in this place. (*She looks at* OLIVE. *Then her eyes fall, ashamed.*)

OLIVE. That's my condition, Jeannie — take it or leave it.

JEANNIE (*desperately*). But I — I must go back, Olive — I must take the money to the club.

OLIVE. What's the name of it?

JEANNIE. The Purple Grotto. Romani Street.

(OLIVE *goes to the trunk down* R. *and takes from it a small tin box, out of which she takes a handful of notes. She counts out some and puts the rest back into the tin, which she replaces in the trunk. For a moment she contemplates this wreckage of her savings. Then she turns and takes her hat and coat from the hook.*)

OLIVE. I'll take the money there myself. You stay here with mother. Sit by the bedside, Jeannie — so she can see you when she wakes up. And you're not to leave her on any account — do you understand?

JEANNIE (*subdued*). Yes, Olive.

(OLIVE, *with a last look at her mother, goes out up* C. JEANNIE *pauses for a moment. Then she hurries to the door, where she stands listening until the slam of the front door is heard. Then she pulls herself together and gives a slight sigh of relief. For a moment she stands in thought, and her gaze strays to the trunk, down* R. *With a quick glance to see that her mother is still sleeping, she goes to the trunk, opens it, takes out the tin box and extracts the remainder of the money. She hastens across to the door, where she pauses and looks back at her mother. With a sudden impulsive movement, she goes to the bed and kisses her mother on the forehead. Then without another look back, she hastens out of the room. There is a slight pause.* MRS MATTHEWS *stirs in her sleep.*)

MRS MATTHEWS (*in her sleep*). Jeannie — Jeannie . . .

CURTAIN.

FURNITURE AND PROPERTY PLOT

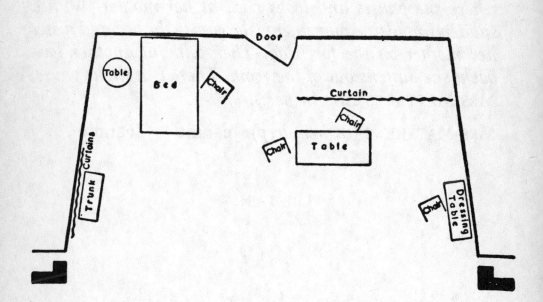

Stage cloth or shabby carpet. Cheap lace curtains down R.
Cheap and shabby curtains drawn across up stage C. to L. to suggest
  a bed hidden there.
1 single bed. Bedclothes cheap but clean and neat.
R. OF BED: small table with medicine, glass, etc.
L. OF BED: chair — small, with arms.
1 small oblong table (L.C.) ON IT: flowers.
2 small chairs at table (R. AND ABOVE).
1 dressing table (USUAL DRESSINGS; DOWN L.).
1 chair at dressing table.
1 small travelling trunk (DOWN R.). IN IT: clothes and other belong-
  ings. Small tin containing treasury notes.

106

PROPERTIES:
OLIVE: a novel, cheap hat and coat on peg (R. WALL).
NURSE: small black bag, containing bottles of medicine, clinical thermometer, and sundries. District nurse's uniform.
JEANNIE: outdoor clothes, cheap and showy. Showy handbag with usual contents.

LIGHTING

FLOATS AND BATTENS: all circuits checked down for subdued light. Gold in battens, and pink in floats, may be somewhat stronger than the other circuits.
INTERIOR BACKING: amber lengths.
NO CUES.

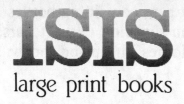

ISIS
large print books

We hope that you have enjoyed this book and will want to read more.

We list some other titles on the next few pages. All our books may be purchased from ISIS at either of the addresses below.

If you are not already a customer, or on our mailing list, please write and ask to be put on the mailing list for regular information about new ISIS titles.

We would also be pleased to receive your suggestions for titles that you would like us to publish in large print. We will look into any suggestions that you send to us.

Happy reading.

ISIS, 55 St Thomas' Street, Oxford OX1 1JG, ENGLAND, tel (0865) 250333

ISIS, ABC – CLIO, 2040 Alameda Padre Serra, PO Box 4397, Santa Barbara, CA 93140 – 4397, USA

SHORT STORIES

Echoes of Laughter

Roald Dahl	**Roald Dahl's Book of Ghost Stories**
Thomas Hardy	**Wessex Tales**
M R James	**A Warning to the Curious**
Barry Pain	**The Eliza Stories**
Saki	**Beasts and Superbeasts**
E OE Somerville and Martin Ross	**Further Experiences of an Irish RM, Volume 2**
E OE Somerville and Martin Ross	**In Mr Knox's Country: An Irish RM, Volume 3**

POETRY AND DRAMA

Lord Birkenhead (Editor)	**John Betjeman's Early Poems**
Joan Duce	**I Remember, I Remember . . .**
Dan Sutherland	**Six Miniatures**

LITERATURE

Leon Garfield	**Shakespeare Stories**

ALSO AVAILABLE IN LARGE PRINT

Longman English Dictionary
Longman Medical Dictionary
Longman Thesaurus
Hammond Large Type World Atlas

Letts Retirement Guides	Finance
Letts Retirement Guides	Good Health
Letts Retirement Guides	House and Garden
Letts Retirement Guides	Leisure and Travel
Robert Dougall	Years Ahead
Margaret Ford	'In Touch' at Home
Consumers Association	Dealing with Household Emergencies
Moyra Bremner	Supertips to Make Life Easy
Rabbi Lionel Blue	Kitchen Blues
William R Hartston	Teach Yourself Chess
Kenneth Beckett	The Love of Gardening
Desmond Morris	Catwatching
Desmond Morris	Dogwatching
Andrew Young	A Prospect of Flowers
Leon Garfield	Shakespeare Stories
Lord Birkenhead (Editor)	John Betjeman's Early Poems
Joan Duce	I Remember, I Remember . . .
Dan Sutherland	Six Miniatures
Beryl Reid	The Cat's Whiskers